Engaging Preschoolers in Mathematics

Engaging Preschoolers in Mathematics is a guide for teachers and childcare professionals working at the Pre-K level that focuses on engagement with the process standards written by the National Council of Teachers of Mathematics. You will learn how to support young children mathematically, use developmentally appropriate mathematical language, and integrate learning activities into your classroom routines that support mathematical content standards. Examples of literacy activities that connect with math are provided throughout the book, as well as learning activities that extend beyond the classroom.

Dr. Jeanne White has been an educator since 1992 when she began teaching elementary school in the south suburbs of Chicago. She is the Director of the Teacher Leadership Graduate Programs at Elmhurst College and teaches math methods courses for early childhood and elementary teacher candidates.

Dr. Linda Dauksas has been teaching and leading programs for young children and families for over thirty-five years. She is the Director of the Early Childhood and Special Education programs at Elmhurst College and teaches assessment and methods courses for early childhood, elementary and special education teacher candidates.

Other Eye On Education Books
Available from Routledge
(www.routledge.com/eyeoneducation)

Engaging Preschoolers in Mathematics

Using Classroom Routines for Problem Solving

Jeanne White and Linda Dauksas

Routledge
Taylor & Francis Group

NEW YORK AND LONDON

First published 2019
by Routledge
711 Third Avenue, New York, NY 10017

and by Routledge
2 Park Square, Milton Park, Abingdon, Oxon, OX14 4RN

Routledge is an imprint of the Taylor & Francis Group, an informa business

Library of Congress Cataloging-in-Publication Data
Names: White, Jeanne (Jeanne Marie), author. | Dauksas, Linda,
author.
Title: Engaging preschoolers in mathematics : using classroom
routines for problem solving / Jeanne White and Linda Dauksas.
Description: New York, NY : Routledge, 2019. | Includes
bibliographical references.
Identifiers: LCCN 2018020392 (print) | LCCN 2018032637 (ebook) |
ISBN 9781315200736 (ebook) | ISBN 9781138710320 (hardback)
| ISBN 9781138710337 (pbk.) | ISBN 9781315200736 (ebk.)
Subjects: LCSH: Mathematics—Study and teaching (Early childhood) |
Mathematics—Study and teaching (Preschool) | Problem solving—
Study and teaching (Early childhood) | Problem solving—Study and
teaching (Preschool)
Classification: LCC QA135.6 (ebook) | LCC QA135.6 .W478 2019
(print) | DDC 372.7/044—dc23
LC record available at https://lccn.loc.gov/2018020392

ISBN: 978-1-138-71032-0 (hbk)
ISBN: 978-1-138-71033-7 (pbk)
ISBN: 978-1-315-20073-6 (ebk)

Typeset in Palatino
by Florence Production Ltd, Stoodleigh, Devon, UK

Contents

Introduction

Engaging Preschoolers in Mathematics

Professionals who work with children in preschool should be engaging children in stimulating mathematical practices on a daily basis. There are burgeoning opportunities for teachers to instill developmentally appropriate problem-solving skills which can set the foundation for critical thinking in mathematics before children enter kindergarten and the primary grades. The National Council of Teachers of Mathematics (NCTM, 2013) advises early childhood educators to introduce math concepts through a variety of experiences to help "children in seeing connections of ideas within mathematics, as well as with other subjects, developing their mathematical knowledge throughout the day and across the curriculum" (p. 2).

Mathematical problem solving can be challenging for young children who are at the beginning stages of learning to read, write, add, and subtract. Preschool teachers can provide developmentally appropriate problem solving as part of daily rituals and routines. As problem solving is promoted, teachers must honor the active and multi-modal nature of young children's learning and remain responsive to their families' context. Teachers will find success if they incorporate mathematics into the existing curriculum for young children. According to the Position Statement *Early childhood mathematics: Promoting good beginnings* (NAEYC, 2010), teachers of 3- to 6-year-old children should engage in the following practices:

In high-quality mathematics education for 3- to 6-year-old children, teachers and other key professionals should:

1. enhance children's natural interest in mathematics and their disposition to use it to make sense of their physical and social worlds;
2. build on children's experience and knowledge, including their family, linguistic, cultural, and community backgrounds; their individual approaches to learning; and their informal knowledge;
3. base mathematics curriculum and teaching practices on knowledge of young children's cognitive, linguistic, physical, and social–emotional development;
4. use curriculum and teaching practices that strengthen children's problem-solving and reasoning processes as well as representing, communicating, and connecting mathematical ideas;
5. ensure that the curriculum is coherent and compatible with known relationships and sequences of important mathematical ideas;
6. provide for children's deep and sustained interaction with key mathematical ideas;
7. integrate mathematics with other activities and other activities with mathematics;
8. actively introduce mathematical concepts, methods, and language through a range of appropriate experiences and teaching strategies;
9. support children's learning by thoughtfully and continually assessing all children's mathematical knowledge, skills, and strategies.

To support high quality mathematics education, institutions, program developers, and policy makers should:

1. create more effective early childhood teacher preparation and continuing professional development;

2. use collaborative processes to develop well-aligned systems of appropriate high-quality standards, curriculum, and assessment;
3. design institutional structures and policies that support teachers' ongoing learning, teamwork, and planning;
4. provide resources necessary to overcome the barriers to young children's mathematical proficiency at the classroom, community, institutional, and system-wide levels.

Used with permission from NAEYC.

Facilitating Engaging Instruction and Multi-Modal Learning

In the context of teaching, active and multi-modal learning refers to practices for young children that promote learning through meaningful, relevant, and authentic experiences with materials in their environments. Children begin to make sense of mathematical vocabulary and concepts when engaging with open-ended, multi-use rich materials during play, physical action, and hands-on experiences. By having interactions with teachers and family members, children engage in mathematical thinking and conversations, generating and asking questions (SCALE, 2016). These learning experiences include multi-sensory approaches such as touching objects as they count, using their body to climb on a chair, and listening for a pattern in a poem.

The intent of this book is to support the design of early learning environments that promote problem solving and mathematical thinking for all young children. Each chapter will include engaging activities that honor the active and multi-modal nature of young children's learning, with the expectation that learning targets should be modified to meet the needs of young children who are learning English, young children who are striving, those performing at an appropriate developmental level, and those performing beyond their chronological age. Because we feel all young children deserve to be included in our classrooms, we made an intentional decision to include strategies and learning activities for all young children in the body of each chapter.

The chapters are organized to include the integration of mathematics across the curriculum as part of daily routines. Mathematics for young children is not limited to a specific time or activity; it must be embedded into the entire day. Mathematics should be apparent in the children's literature used in the curriculum, echoed in daily rituals, evidenced in all areas of the learning environments inside and outside of the school building, and shared with families to reinforce learning.

There are five chapters in this book: one to explain the process standards established by the National Council of Teachers of Mathematics (NCTM, 2000), and four content chapters: number sense; patterns and number relationships; measurement; and geometry. The chapters are not sequential, so teachers can use all or part of a content chapter based on the curriculum as well as what is developmentally appropriate for the learners in their classroom. Learning targets for preschoolers are included in each chapter, written in child-friendly language so teachers can explain the targets to children and their families. Each chapter includes several children's literature books and hands-on manipulative materials that can be used to facilitate the process standards as well as promote mathematical concepts. Suggested book titles and materials for each content area are included in the last chapter. The Appendix includes sample activity plans for each content area so teachers can easily create plans for embedding mathematics into routines such as snack, the sensory table, outdoor plan, and circle time.

Assessing Active Learning

All learning for young children should align with appropriate assessments. According to the NAEYC Position Statement *Where we stand on curriculum, assessment and program evaluation* (2009), "to best assess young children's strengths, progress, and needs, use assessment methods that are developmentally appropriate, culturally and linguistically responsive, tied to children's daily activities, supported by professional development, inclusive of families, and connected to specific, beneficial purposes (p. 1)."

Before teachers design learning for young children, they need to collect data from multiple sources in order to make decisions regarding learning targets and objectives. Teachers and other adults in the setting should use a variety of observation strategies including photos, videos, audio recordings, anecdotal records, checklists, time samples, student work, and curriculum-based assessments to document children's abilities related to the content areas for mathematics. The type of data collected should align with the skills being assessed, yet be an efficient way of collecting the data. For example, anecdotal recordings provide detail and allow for elaboration, but are time consuming for adults to complete. Taking photos of children's work may be a more efficient way to collect data and document the work of several young children at the same time.

Another example of collecting data for the entire class would be to use a class observation log. Teachers can set a class observation log with each child's name on a clipboard in each center or area of the room. Each log sheet should have the date and should define the math skill and criteria needed to assess the students. There should be a place for the adult completing the log sheet to initial the assessment. After children practice a particular skill for a number of days, the data sheets should be reviewed to determine understandings, misunderstandings, and next steps for planning instruction. As children engage in daily play and exploration, adults can document performance and growth toward skill development. Teachers must also collect data specific to any Individualized Educational Plans in order to document children's progress toward goals.

A collection of different types of artifacts should be compiled into a portfolio for each child. The portfolio should illustrate growth and provide the audience of readers with the scope of content presented to young children. When creating portfolios, teachers should also date each artifact, link it to the appropriate standard and skill, and include a statement of progress or performance for the audience of readers.

Using Children's Literature with Mathematical Concepts

Throughout the book, the intentional selection of children's literature reinforces mathematical concepts, integrates content across the curriculum, and honors the diversity of today's families, schools, and communities. We know children perform better when teachers are responsive to their needs and when classroom materials are reflective of children and their families. This book intends to do both, while supporting mathematical thinking by young children. The book is intended for teachers of young children with varying abilities, as well as children who are learning English. The literature selections support the need for active and multi-modal learning. Young children are allowed to see themselves and their families in these selections through illustrations, setting, text features, or problems presented.

Teachers can integrate mathematical problem solving into the curriculum using children's literature as the context. Teachers can relate mathematical concepts to illustrations from the book and use characters and role-playing from the story to create problems for children to solve. Using literature that illustrates the children's families, cultures, first languages, and communities makes the application of concepts more meaningful for young children. When teachers incorporate children's literature into mathematics, opportunities arise for young children to see math in their own lives. If they see how characters in a story use math to solve problems, they can better understand how people around them use math to solve everyday problems.

Reinforcing Appropriate Mathematical Vocabulary

Each chapter includes examples of developmentally appropriate vocabulary that correspond with the mathematical concepts.

It is suggested that teachers share these vocabulary words, as well as how they are used, with families. In order to promote an early and accurate understanding of mathematical concepts, teachers, children, and families must use the correct mathematical terms. For example, a ball should be described as a *sphere*, even though it appears as a circle when shown as an illustration or drawn on paper. Terminology should be consistent so when children move to kindergarten and primary grades their understandings are accurate. For example, young children should be taught to use the terms *greater than* and *less than*, rather than words such as *big number* or *little number*, to compare quantities. Most importantly, in order to reinforce the meaning of mathematical concepts, new vocabulary must be taught as part of the instruction. Suggestions for teaching the meaning of these new words are included in each chapter, based on the *Say-Tell-Do-Play* strategy created by the Southwest Institute for Families & Children (www.swifamilies.org). This strategy can be used by families with their child by pairing an action with each word and providing opportunities for children to reinforce the meaning of each word in multiple ways.

Using the Environment to Promote Mathematical Problem Solving

In each content chapter, examples are provided for creating a mathematical environment in areas typically found in a preschool setting: block center; dramatic play area; sensory table; art center, manipulative center; and snack time. As a result, the environment places an emphasis on the importance of mathematics to young children and others who visit or work in the classroom. In order to encourage the active, multi-modal nature of young children's learning, math and literacy should be evident in every corner of the classroom. When working with young children the environment is said to be the third teacher, so it is essential that the floor map, furnishings, materials, and displays promote the learning of mathematics.

Since the creation of the environment is deliberate, teachers must ensure that every student moves through the classroom interacting with materials in all areas as part of their daily routine. As one of the guidelines for including academic content in early childhood programs, teachers and curriculum directors should "select important, appropriate academic content" with activities that connect not only with the children's abilities but with their interests as well (Hyson, 2003, p. 21). Teachers should allow time for children to engage in various activities and allow them to return to those activities that generate high interest. The environment should also be structured to provide time for teachers to observe and collect data to describe each child's progress toward goals and objectives. Many early learning curricula are theme-based. The four content areas in this book can be easily integrated into a variety of curriculum themes or topics. A sample learning environment plan is included in each chapter.

Beyond the Classroom

Each chapter includes activities to share with families, extending children's learning beyond the classroom. The suggestions should be shared via newsletters, blogs, or websites to deepen both children's and families' understandings of mathematical concepts that can be explored before children reach kindergarten. The types of family activities we have included do not rely on technology, which may not be accessible for all families, but involve the use of household objects and natural routines. A sample newsletter is included at the end of each content chapter with mathematical vocabulary and suggested home activities that build on the classroom activities.

Teachers can extend the mathematical concepts beyond the classroom by offering opportunities for families to participate in events held at the school or a local site such as a public library, YMCA, or park district. School members can host make-and-take workshops, where families can create materials to practice math concepts at home, or plan activities in a gym or other large space where families can use manipulatives and equipment with their child to engage in math-related activities.

Making the Most of this Book

This book is written for professionals working with young children to expose and prepare their students to engage in problem solving as a part of their daily routines at school and at home. Teachers and childcare professionals should use the book to learn about the NCTM process standards, developmentally appropriate mathematical language, learning activities that support mathematical concepts, and examples of literacy activities to connect with math concepts, as well as activities for families that extend beyond the classroom.

1

1

Applying the Mathematical Process Standards

The National Council of Teachers of Mathematics has established five process standards that children should use to acquire and apply mathematical content knowledge: problem solving, reasoning and proof, communication, connections, and representations. These five process standards are intended to be introduced in prekindergarten and used through grade 12 (NCTM, 2000).

As young children learn skills and strategies for adding and subtracting, they must also learn how to connect mathematical problems to what they know and communicate why they are solving problems in a particular way, as well as how to represent the problem and its solution. Teachers of young children should look for opportunities to introduce these process standards to their students in order to set the foundation for critical thinking with regard to mathematics in preschool, kindergarten, and beyond.

Teachers can work with colleagues to convey the process standards in child-friendly language, then decide how to gradually incorporate these standards into the math curriculum. The process standards can be introduced by building on routine activities and using familiar stories and situations in the children's environment.

Problem Solving

In order for young children to make sense of a problem, they have to understand the words, symbols, and numbers in the problem. Teachers can start gradually by sharing a math problem introduced in a familiar story, daily routine, or children's book. The teacher can state the problem along with pictures and numbers and ask for a child to explain the problem in their own words. Children can use objects and illustrations, or draw a picture, to represent the problem or situation and learn how their peers solved the same problem.

Young children can be introduced to the problem-solving process standard using the following *I Can* statements:

◆ *I can discover a math problem.*
◆ *I can use words and pictures to solve a math problem.*
◆ *I can show others how I solved a math problem.*

Introducing the Problem-Solving Standard

Use a selection of children's literature with which children are familiar such as *Five little monkeys jumping on the bed* (Christelow, 1989). Let the children know there is a math problem in the story and you need their help to solve the problem. Start reading the story but stop after the first monkey falls off the bed and ask, "There were some monkeys jumping on the bed. One fell off the bed. I am wondering, how many monkeys are on the bed now?" Write the statement *I can discover a math problem*, and tell the children they will be able to talk to their friends how many monkeys are on the bed now. Then provide the children with a simple drawing of a bed with five circle stickers. Each sticker represents a monkey. Allow the children to peel off one sticker at a time as the monkeys fall off the bed. Or, depending on the children's abilities, have them draw the five monkeys on the bed (you can model how to draw circles to represent the monkeys) and then read the math problem again. Write the statement *I can use words and pictures to solve a math problem*, and tell the children they can figure out how many monkeys are on the bed using words and the stickers or picture they drew of the five monkeys on the bed. Let a few children show their representations and explain how they know how many monkeys are on the bed after one fell off. Write the statement *I can show others how I solved a math problem*, and let the children know they will show their picture to a partner and tell each other how many monkeys are on the bed after one fell off.

Representations

Children are exposed to problem solving in preschool with toys, blocks, or props for dramatic play. When children are in kindergarten, they begin to move away from the concrete stage of learning and begin to pair symbols with objects or drawings to represent problem-solving situations. Teachers can gradually model this connecting stage in which young children use physical and visual representations to be able to successfully reach the abstract stage in later grades.

Young children can be introduced to the representations process standard using the following *I Can* statements:

◆ *I can use real objects to solve problems.*
◆ *I can use pictures of objects to solve problems.*
◆ *I can begin to use symbols to solve problems.*

Introducing the Representations Standard

Write the statement *I can use real objects to* solve *problems,* and introduce the book *The very hungry caterpillar* (Carle, 1969). Have food to represent the fruit in the story and demonstrate how the caterpillar ate through one apple, two pears, three plums, four strawberries, and five oranges. Ask different questions such as, "How many pieces of fruit did the caterpillar eat altogether on Monday and Tuesday? Let's count the fruit." Then count the fruit with the class to solve the problem.

On another day, write the statement *I can use pictures of objects to solve problems,* and revisit the lesson when the children counted the fruit to solve the problems from *The very hungry caterpillar.* Instead of using the actual fruit, children can use stickers, pictures, or drawings (depending on the students' abilities) of fruit to solve the problems. Use the same problems or create new ones about how many pieces of fruit the caterpillar ate in the story. Let children show their representations and explain how they know how many pieces of fruit the caterpillar ate.

When students are ready to move away from physical and pictorial representations, write the statement *I can begin to use symbols to solve problems*. Tell the children you are going to model for them how to use counters to solve a problem. Revisit the problem-solving sessions with the caterpillar and the fruit by stating, "First we counted pieces of fruit and then we used pictures of the fruit. Now we are going to use counters as the fruit to solve the math problems." Give each student a container with counters and pose the problem, "On Friday, the caterpillar ate through five oranges. Using the counters, show me how many oranges the caterpillar ate on Friday," and have children count out five counters. Create other math problems from the story using the counters to represent the fruit.

Connections

Young children in early grades are starting to see how word problems are connected to their daily lives. They can identify numbers in a math problem and are starting to use their knowledge of quantity as well as math vocabulary to solve a problem. Teachers can create opportunities for children to use math to solve problems that connect to their lives at home and at school. In addition, teachers can help students make connections between activities such as sorting blocks at school with sorting clothes at home.

Young children can be introduced to the communication process standard using the following *I Can* statements:

◆ *I can use math to solve problems at school.*
◆ *I can use math to solve problems at home.*
◆ *I can use math to solve problems when I play.*

Introducing the Connections Standard

Write the statement *I can use math to solve problems about school*. Let the children know there are many times when they can use math to solve a problem at school. Use examples such as a table with chairs and ask, "How can I figure out how many people can sit at this table when we have snack?" Talk about how you can count the number of chairs at the table and that is how many people can sit at that table. Use other situations such as the number of snacks needed for a group or whether more chairs can fit around a square or a circular table.

Let the children know they can also use math to solve a problem at home as you write the statement *I can use math to solve problems about home*. Have the children draw pictures of the people in their household. Then ask questions such as, "Are there more children or more adults? How many chairs will we need so everyone can sit together at a table to eat dinner?" Then write the statement *I can use math to solve problems when I play*. Have children count the number of a particular toy (cars, play figures, etc.) in the classroom and tell them you are going to send home a note about counting the same category of toy at home. Provide problem-solving opportunities in school once a week that correspond to activities at home and put these in the weekly newsletter.

Reasoning and Proof

Young children can be taught at an early age to justify their answers, as well as share their reasoning with others, so they can start to build a repertoire of strategies and get in the habit of producing an explanation. Children can use objects, illustrations, pictures, or actions to explain their thinking, as a way to share their answers with peers. They can also practice their social skills by learning how to listen when others are explaining how they solved a problem.

Young children can be introduced to the reasoning and proof process standard using the following *I Can* statements:

◆ *I can share my answer using math words.*
◆ *I can listen to how my friends solved the same problem.*
◆ *I can solve math problems in more than one way.*

Introducing the Reasoning and Proof Standard

Using the book *Five little monkeys jumping on the bed* again, write the statement *I can share my answer using math words*. Remind the children how they have been using objects, illustrations, and drawing pictures to figure out how many monkeys were on the bed after each one fell off. Ask the children which words they used to tell their partner about the math problem with the monkeys (possible responses: *monkeys, count, fell, number, five, four, three, two, one*). Have the children practice using each suggested math vocabulary word to share their answer. Listen for students who are using the vocabulary correctly and have them model how they shared their answer using sentences with each of the math words.

Tell the children they are going to practice being a good listener when their partner tells them how they solved the problem. Write the statement *I can listen to how my friends solved the same problem*. Give some guidelines for listening such as *I can look at my friend when they are talking* and *I can wait for my turn to talk*. Have the children practice using the guidelines for listening as they tell each other how they solved the same math problem. Then talk about the different examples of how the problem was solved and write *I can solve math problems in more than one way*. Provide frequent opportunities for children to share their math ideas with friends and tell the class how they can solve math problems that arise in the classroom, such as figuring out how many chairs they need to fit around a table.

Communication

When teachers ask children how they arrived at their answer they often hear, "I just knew it" or "that was the number in my head." Typically, young children have difficulty verbalizing their solution process. In order to provide an explanation, a child must have a model of what to say along with strong content knowledge, which includes the use of correct mathematical vocabulary.

Young children in preschool are learning to use mathematical vocabulary in a word problem when they hear their teacher or other adults use these terms. They are being introduced to problem-solving strategies such as drawing a picture, which they can use to imitate problem solving after much modeling and thinking aloud demonstrated by the teacher.

Young children can be introduced to the communication process standard using the following *I Can* statements:

◆ *I can imitate problem solving.*
◆ *I can label my math drawings.*
◆ *I can use math words to solve a problem.*

Introducing the Communication Standard

Remind children of the math problem involving the five little monkeys, or choose a similar story to create a new math problem such as *Five little monkeys sitting in a tree* (Christelow, 1993). Write the statement *I can imitate problem solving*, and explain that you want them to repeat what you say as you solve the problem in the story. For example, as you show the illustration, start by saying, "I see five monkeys in the tree," and have children repeat. Then say, "I see one monkey fell out of the tree," and have children repeat. Then say, "Now I will count the monkeys still in the tree. One, two, three, four," and have children repeat. Finally, "I know there are four monkeys in the tree because I counted them," and have children repeat.

Write the statement *I can label my math drawings*. Model for the children how they can write a number above each of the five monkeys so they can label the monkeys in the drawings. Then, when one of the monkeys falls off the bed, or out of the tree, they can cross out the monkey with the five above it.

Write the statement *I can use math words to solve a problem*. After they have crossed out the monkey with the five above it, tell them to look at their drawing now. They can tell their partner what they see on their drawing. For example, "There is one monkey and the number five is crossed off. There are monkeys that are still on the bed (or in the tree). I can see the numbers one through four on the other monkeys." Ask the children, how many monkeys are there now? Model how they can talk about the monkeys they drew and the numbers above the remaining monkeys to find their answer.

Wrapping Up

Teachers can introduce the five process standards to young children in a way that builds on what they already know and connects to math content and skills established in the curriculum. Children can also use familiar stories, objects, and pictures to learn how to apply these five process standards throughout their daily routines. Teachers can help students connect mathematical problem solving at home and school by providing activities that can occur in both settings, and by asking families to share experiences involving math from their daily lives that provide opportunities for applying the process standards.

2

2

Establishing Problem-Solving Routines to Promote Number Sense

Numbers are ever present in the daily routines of young children. Throughout their days, young children have opportunities to count in fun and meaningful ways. We hear children count how many friends came to school or how many stayed home, the number of blocks in a tower, the number of cookies on a plate, the number of times they jump in the air, or the number of books read during story time.

In addition to counting, young children are fascinated by who has *more* of their favorite things as they become attentive to the distribution of objects to be sure quantities are "fair." These initial observations of the world are mathematical at their core because they are about quantity. Children can apply problem-solving strategies, such as acting out a problem or drawing a picture, as they move from counting objects up to five then eventually up to ten.

The following skills are introduced in this chapter:

◆ recite numbers one to ten;
◆ subitize up to four objects;

- count with understanding in sets up to five;
- connect numbers to quantities using objects and pictures;
- compare two groups using *more, less, equal, same*;
- differentiate numbers from letters or other symbols.

Problem Solving with Number Sense

In order to make sense of counting, young children use movement, hands-on materials, and pictures to display their understanding of these mathematical concepts, including marks or drawings to represent a quantity. Likewise, young children will use their own visual representations and real objects to enhance their understanding of *how many*. When talking about quantities, teachers can present small objects for children to hold and manipulate to represent a number. These kinesthetic and visual representations will allow children to feel and see the meaning of these quantities. Teachers should provide opportunities for children to solve problems that arise in the context of the classroom routines and the typical school day using the following *I Can* statements:

- *I can discover how to solve a problem by counting.*
- *I can use words and pictures to solve a problem.*
- *I can show others how I solved a problem using numbers.*

Children can be exposed to numbers in written and spoken form, in English and in their home language. Many children, or their families, may know how to say numbers up to ten in an additional language. It is important to continually ask children, *How many?* with many types of objects, starting with up to three objects, then gradually adding one more. Children can discover how to solve a problem by counting objects such as children, chairs or toys. Pose a question such as, "How many chairs do we need at this table for Max, Cormac and Ella?" Talk about how to decide the number of chairs needed by first counting the number of children. Look for opportunities for children to practice subitizing up to four, which means they can recognize how many in a set without counting.

Then move onto posing problems children can solve using words and pictures. Ask the class, how many friends can sit together at the tables. They can draw a picture to represent the table and chairs and then tell an adult about their drawing. Once they have done similar activities, have children show their picture to peers and tell them what they drew.

Representing Number Sense with Literacy

Teachers can provide experiences with books that allow for demonstrating various concepts related to number sense, such as counting and identifying numbers. The use of children's literature can facilitate the application of the following *I Can* statements:

- ◆ *I can use real objects to solve counting problems.*
- ◆ *I can use pictures of objects to solve counting problems.*
- ◆ *I can begin to use symbols to solve counting problems.*

Pete the cat and his four groovy buttons (2012) by Eric Litwin is one book in a series that allows the reader to make text-to-text connections about the problem-solving nature and perseverance of the main character, Pete the cat. In this story, Pete puts on his favorite shirt and sings, "My buttons, my buttons, my four groovy buttons." Allow children to show their understanding of subitizing by acting out the story using paper buttons taped to their shirt. When Pete loses his button, the children can remove one of their paper buttons and count the remaining buttons in order to figure out the question at the bottom of the page, "How many buttons are left?" Continue until all of Pete's buttons are gone, then have children put all four buttons back on their shirt and retell the story while they act it out again. This book can then be used to practice subitizing. Show Pete with various numbers of buttons from the story and see if the children can tell you how many buttons he is wearing without counting them.

After reading the story, make a class book based on the pattern in the story. Complete the sentence for each child and compile the pages into a book accompanied by the children's illustrations: _____ has _____buttons on his/her_____. Children can use the character of Pete the cat throughout the year to create stories of their own involving objects from his books. They can draw a picture or use stickers or stamps of Pete with up to ten objects and include a sentence describing their illustration, such as *Pete the cat found 4 shells on the beach.*

Read other books about buttons to create a week-long theme with buttons. Children can identify the main character in each book, answer questions about each story, and count the number of buttons on each page. Place the following books in respective centers throughout the classroom: dramatic play—*Corduroy* (1976) by Don Freeman; manipulative center—*10 button book* (1999) by William Accorsi; sensory table—*The button box* (1990) by Margarette S. Reid; gross motor—*Counting by tens* (2006) by Michael Dahl.

Children can make individual counting books with their objects of choice to reinforce counting. For example, a child may choose to make a counting book about a red hat. The child would use stickers or stamps, or draw one red hat, on the first page and dictate her sentence to an adult—for example, *There is one red hat* or *one hat.* Each child can make as many pages in their personal counting book as is appropriate for their development. Then show two pages and have children compare the quantities shown on the pages, using the words *more*, *less*, and *same.*

Remain mindful when selecting children's literature that not all counting books are suitable for rational counting, i.e., assigning a number to the objects counted. Some counting books include a variety of objects on each page which can distract children from the quantity, so they focus on non-essential attributes of objects such as color, size, or shape. Other counting books include objects on the page in addition to the objects being counted, so children are not able to understand the connection between the number and the quantity of objects on each page. The book *Ten black dots* (1968) by Donald Crews is appropriate for teaching the concept of rational counting, as well as providing practice for counting objects in various arrangements. Each page has the corresponding number of black dots so the child only pays attention to the numeral and the quantity. Children can then make their own picture using black Bingo daubers to make dots and then dictate a sentence about their picture, such as *three black dots are buttons.*

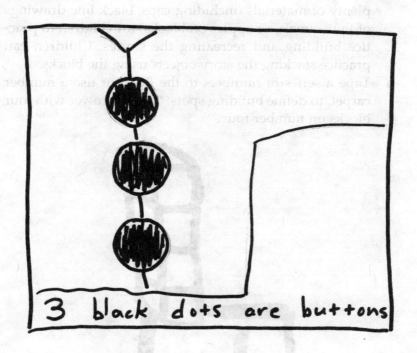

Connecting Number Sense to the Environment

Teachers can create classroom activities and centers for guided and independent practice of counting concepts to honor the active and multi-modal nature of young children's learning. By varying the types of activities each day, all children will have engaged in several counting activities by the end of the week. Children should be encouraged to use their home language to count. Children should count objects and people in their environment and be exposed to numbers in various settings, such as symbols that may appear outside the building (address), outside a classroom (room numbers), or on signage in the environment.

In the block center:

◆ Place *Caps for sale* (1940), *The napping house* (1984), or *Ten apples up on top!* (1961) in a block center. Provide plenty of materials (including caps, black line drawings of the animals, or apples on blocks) for children to practice building and recreating the stories. Children can practice stacking the story objects using the blocks.

◆ Tape a series of numbers to the floor, or use a number carpet, to define building spots: "Build a tower with four blocks on number four."

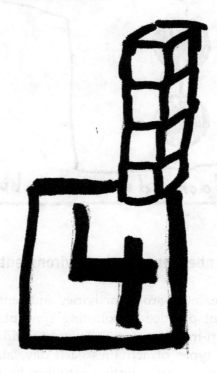

In the dramatic play center:

◆ Place the book *Feast for 10* (1993) in the dramatic play area. Provide pretend food and props to allow children to recreate the story and shop for a feast. Create a set of cards, plates, bowls, muffin tins, egg cartons, plastic eggs, sand buckets, or other small containers with numerals printed on them. Provide small manipulatives such as blocks, cubes, pom poms, plastic bugs, shells, sticks, or stones and allow children to match manipulatives to quantity.

◆ Set up a fishing pond (plastic pool or sensory tub); add magnetic numbers and fishing poles. When a number is "caught" the child can practice reciting numbers starting with that number. Add magnetic letters to the pond, instructing the children to fish only for numbers.

At the sensory table or in a sensory bin:

◆ Children can trace numbers with their finger in sand, in shaving cream, or in hair gel enclosed in a plastic sandwich bag. Emphasize the differences between the 2 and 5 and the 6 and 9, which children often confuse in their writing.

◆ Have a variety of large sets of numbers 0–9 (plastic, magnetic, wooden) in the center. Children can find the same numeral from the different sets.

◆ Fill the table with numbers and letters and instruct children to find only the numbers.

◆ Provide sets of objects that can be grouped, such as Learning Links hooked together, connected Unifix cubes, beads on a chenille stem, and buttons in a paper baking cup. Children can use the same materials to create their own sets of up to five, counting out each Link, Unifix cube, bead, or button as they make their set.

At the art center:

◆ Provide materials such as play dough and chenille stems along with numeral cards up to nine. Children can use the pliable materials to create each numeral.

◆ Children can use Bingo daubers to recreate the story *Ten black dots* by dabbing one dot on a piece of paper and making the dot into an object or person. Then do the same with two dots up through ten, or to a quantity appropriate for the child.

At the manipulative center:

◆ Use a large set of dice and tell the children the dots on each side are buttons. Each child can roll one die and see if he/she can identify the number of "buttons" on the side facing up without counting. Using Duplo blocks, each child can match the number of Duplo blocks to the number of "buttons" on the face of the die, then build a tower with the corresponding quantity. Children can compare towers with a friend to see which tower has more.

◆ Create a set of 5 × 7 inch cards with stickers, putting one sticker on a card, two stickers on another card, up to ten stickers on a card (each sticker should be the same design). Children can match a numeral card to the appropriate sticker card. Differentiate the number of cards for different children, starting with cards up to the quantity five then gradually adding one or two more sets of cards.

◆ Create a set of 5 × 7 inch cards with a numeral and the corresponding number of dots for numbers one through five. Mix them up and have children put them in order. Gradually add one more numeral/dot card until they can go up to 20.

At snack time:

◆ Use number symbols to label tables or chairs in the classroom. Tell children to sit at a specific table or chair for snack: "Tom, please sit at table 2."
◆ Reinforce terms such as *more, less, same,* and *equal* when eating a snack by asking, "You have four crackers left. Who has the *same* number of crackers? Who has *less*?" or "Can you find two people who have an *equal* number of crackers?"
◆ Put out a variety of snacks and let children try one of each. Then each child can ask for the snack they liked the best: "May I please have *more* grapes?"

Below is a sample of areas in the classroom that can be designed to foster independent practice of counting.

Reasoning and Proof via Exploration of Number Sense

Children can begin to explore the reasoning behind counting concepts, as well as prove their answer is correct, by applying the following *I Can* statements:

◆ *I can share my answer using math vocabulary words.*
◆ *I can listen to how my friends counted the same objects.*
◆ *I can count objects in more than one way.*

In addition to using centers for independent practice, be sure to rotate the children in order to work and explore number concepts with a partner or as a member of a small group to

Blocks	Dramatic Play	Manipulatives
Add a variety of blocks including cardboard blocks, waffle blocks, wooden blocks, and foam blocks to the area. Designate a number for play or for each day. Have children practice building structures with that number of pieces.	Play and retell counting stories with dramatic play materials. For example: *Ten apples up on top!*, *Feast for 10*, or *Caps for sale* provide appropriate counting practice with props.	Provide number cards and ask the children to match the number with the appropriate quantity of manipulatives (Unifix cubes, teddy bear counters, buttons, etc.)
Easel	Sensory Table	Writing
Place large cut out numbers on the easel. Children can fill them with corresponding number of paint blobs. For example, a child would add seven blobs of paint on the number 7.	Place numbered containers (cups, tubs) or chenille sticks in the sensory table with objects or beads. Allow children to fill each container or cover the stick with the matching number of objects or beads.	Use your fingers to practice writing number symbols in salt or sand trays. Add number signs and magnetic numbers as needed for visual samples.
Gross Motor	Snack	Outdoors
Create an extra-large number line on the floor with tape and laminated numbers. Have children pick a number from a pile and ask them to count and move (hop, crawl, slither, walk backwards, etc.) to the designated number.	Add numbers to your paper plates or on laminated placemats. Have children serve themselves the appropriate number of items to correspond with the number on the plate or mat.	Go on a number hunt. Hunt for a designated number on buildings or signs. Be sure to take photos of children with the numbers they find and display them in the classroom or post them on your website.

enhance their counting skills. When children work with others they can practice checking and explaining quantities with their peers.

When distributing or sharing materials with peers, young children will be able to observe quantities for fairness. They will be able to practice using vocabulary and comparing quantities. Show children two groups of objects (no more than five or six in each group) and ask them "Which one has more?," allowing them to count the objects so they can justify their answer by comparing them. As children are lining up, ask if there are more bus riders or more walkers in line, then have the children count the number of children in each group to justify their answer.

Allow children to count a group of objects in more than one way. For example, line up four toy cars and have the children count them as you touch each car. Then rearrange the cars and ask if anyone knows how many cars there are now. Count them again to check to see if there are still four. Do the same type of activity with a different group of objects another day, keeping track of who is able to tell you that there are the same number of objects regardless of the arrangement.

Communication of Number Sense among Young Children

Children should use play, snack, and group time to practice using academic language for mathematics each day. The vocabulary related to number sense includes: *more, less, same, equal, just one, one more*. Young children can communicate about number sense when they apply the following *I Can* statements:

- ◆ *I can imitate comparing groups.*
- ◆ *I can use drawings to show numbers.*
- ◆ *I can use math vocabulary to solve a problem.*

Find classroom materials that you can compare, such as crayons and markers. Demonstrate how you can compare the groups by counting the number of objects in each group. At first, compare groups that have the same number. For example, show three crayons and three markers. Tell the class you want to know if there are *more* crayons, *more* markers, or if there is the *same* number of crayons as markers. Count the crayons and write "3 crayons" on the board or chart paper. Count the markers and write "3 markers." Then say, "There are three crayons and three markers, so there is the *same* number of crayons as markers. Now I want you to try it." Give children three crayons and three markers and have them count the crayons then the markers, repeating your words. Then add *one more* to a set, and count them again, using a number line (from 0 to 10) to find the two numbers and have children tell you which group has *more*.

Children can use drawings to represent quantities as well as practice writing numbers up to five. Using characters, such as Pete the cat, or objects, such as black dots, from the children's literature, encourage children to draw circles on their paper to represent buttons or dots. They can draw one circle at the top of their paper and write a 1 next to it. Then they can draw two circles below and write a 2 next to it, and so on until they have five circles.

The vocabulary related to number sense should become a part of your daily routines and be used to solve everyday problems. For example, ask the class, "Students who wore boots today will have to line up first in order to change into their shoes. Did *more* students wear boots or shoes today?" As a class, count the number of students who wore boots and write that number on the board. Then count the number of students who wore shoes and write that number on the board. Have the class tell you which group has *more* or if there is the *same* number.

Partnering with Families and Community

Families can extend the activities and build on the concepts at home when they have examples of the concepts related to number sense. They should also be aware of the types of activities completed with household objects, while traveling or when they are in their communities. Share titles of counting books and send home class-made counting books from your classroom.

Families should be included in planning family workshops that reinforce number sense. For example, host a play dough workshop where families can share recipes for different types of play dough and select one recipe to make their own. Then they can work with their child to create symbols and match quantities of objects using the dough. Provide number cards so children can use the symbols on the cards as a model for making and matching dough symbols. Create balls or snakes out of the dough to match the quantity to the number on each card. Another workshop idea is to have families make simple games. Families can teach each other to make games that provide practice in matching numbers or quantities of objects to numbers using materials such as pom poms, beads, or stickers.

In order to practice number sense in the community, encourage families to visit different parks and playgrounds in their neighborhood. Count the swings, slides, and ladders at each site. Be sure to encourage families to compare quantities using mathematical vocabulary such as *more*, *less*, and *same*.

Below is a sample newsletter you can create for families so they can continue to practice the math concepts and skills at home. Or you can include a math section into your current family newsletter.

Weekly Newsletter

Practice these math activities with your child in daily routines outside of school.

Topic: Counting

Vocabulary

Vocabulary words: **How many?**, **more** (greater number), **less** (smaller number), **same** (not different), **equal** (same number), **just one** (a single object), **one more** (adding one to a set).

1. Create word cards with your child. Look at the word cards and *say* the words.

2. As your child looks at the words, have him/her *tell* a family member what the word card says.

3. Your child will show you how to *do* the word card by performing an action when shown the word card. For example, say, "I have two buttons. You have three buttons. You have **more** buttons." while the child puts his hands wider.

4. Duplicate the word cards and *play* a memory matching game.

Spill four objects, such as Cheerios, on a table and ask, "**How many?**" Have your child count them. Then put two Cheerios in front of you and ask, "Do we have the **same** number of Cheerios?" Have your child count the Cheerios in each group.

At Home

Identify quantities up to five, such as cookies on a plate. Look for opportunities to compare quantities and reinforce the vocabulary words. For example, you can point to a row of socks and say, "There are four socks." Then point to another row and say, "There are six socks. There are **more** socks in this row."

When going up and down stairs, count the number of stairs. When outside walking, count your steps to a specific destination (bus stop, to a friend's apartment, etc).

Count the number of plates and cups needed when setting the table and count them as your child sets each piece on the table.

At Play

Count the number of blocks used to build a tower or the number of toys, such as cars or dolls, lined up in a row.

Take pictures of objects that represent the quantities one through ten, such as one cat, two cups, three toys, etc., and email them or bring them to school. We will print and post them in our classroom on our bulletin board.

On the Go

Search for numbers in your neighborhood. Look at the numbers on signs or in a store. Try to find numbers 1 through 10 in a single day.

Books about counting to check out at the library:

Pete the cat and his four groovy buttons—Litwin
Ten black dots—Crews
Feast for 10—Falwell
Caps for sale—Slobodkina

Looking Ahead

The learning activities in this chapter can strengthen young children's counting skills and number sense. These skills can be defined as learning targets. Learning targets should be posted in your classroom for children and visitors to be made aware of the learning that is taking place. The targets should be shared with families to reinforce their understanding of learning activities in the classroom.

The following *I Can* statements are suggestions for learning targets and should be tailored to your children's abilities:

◆ *I can say numbers up to ten.*
◆ *I can write my numbers to 5.*
◆ *I can count objects up to five.*
◆ *I can count to answer "How many?"*
◆ *I can see if a group has the same or more.*

3

Establishing Problem-Solving Routines to Promote Patterns and Number Relationships

Once young children can count to ten, and for some children, up to twenty, they can begin to further explore numbers to see patterns and relationships. These relationships might be visual, such as when children begin to notice that numbers 11 through 19 have a "1" as the first digit and the second digit counts up from 1 to 9. They can use children's literature stories and hands-on activities to begin breaking down large numbers into smaller numbers, such as seeing five as two and three. This can lead to opportunities to introduce complements of ten, as well as concepts of addition and subtraction with small numbers of objects while using real-world examples in the classroom and at home.

Another concept young children can begin to explore in preschool is pattern exploration. Young children should explore patterns using multi-modal activities in their environment and eventually be exposed to patterns within the counting system.

Children can explore patterns with numbers as they learn to count by twos, fives and tens.

The following skills will be included in this chapter:

◆ add one more to a group;
◆ break down a number into groups;
◆ learn complements of ten;
◆ take one away from a group;
◆ copy, describe, extend, and create a pattern with various modalities;
◆ notice patterns in numbers and skip counting.

Problem Solving with Patterns and Number Relationships

Teachers should provide opportunities for children to solve problems about patterns and number relationships that arise in the context of classroom routines and the typical school day using the following *I Can* statements:

◆ *I can discover problems about adding or taking away.*
◆ *I can use words and pictures to solve math problems by adding or taking away.*
◆ *I can tell others how to solve math problems by adding or taking away.*

Set up opportunities for children to see problems involving math that can occur within the classroom, such as setting up tables for activities. Intentionally omit a table so children can see there are not enough tables for everyone to sit. Ask children if they can discover the problem with the number of tables for the activities. Prompt children, if needed, to articulate the problem— There are not enough tables for everyone to sit for our activity. Then children can use words as well as pictures to solve the problem which involves adding *one more* to a group of objects. For example, they can draw two squares to represent tables in the classroom and count "*one, two*" after they draw the squares.

Have the children tell you we need one more table for the classroom, then prompt them to draw one more square in their picture. Ask them to tell you how many tables there are now by counting the squares in their new picture: *"one, two, three."* Children can show others how they solved the problem by sharing their drawing with their friends and telling them how they found the answer. Conduct a similar activity where you have too many objects and you need the children to help you solve the problem involving taking away an object.

Representing Patterns and Number Relationships with Literacy

Teachers can provide experiences with books that allow for representation of number relationships and exploration of patterns. The use of children's literature can facilitate the application of the following *I Can* statements:

- ◆ *I can use objects or pictures from books to solve problems about adding.*
- ◆ *I can use objects or pictures from books to solve problems about subtracting.*
- ◆ *I can use object or pictures from books to solve problems about patterns.*

Young children can begin exploring number relationships using Greg Tang's books, *Math fables* (2004) and *Math fables too* (2007), which use pictures of animals to demonstrate how numbers can be broken down into groups. For example, five raccoons are shown as a group of two and three, and a group of one and four. The book *Seven blind mice* (Young, 1992) is based on the Asian folktale in which seven blind mice take turns going to the pond to feel the strange something, until they put their ideas together and realize it is an elephant. Children can use counters to represent the way the mice separate from the group as one and six, two and five, etc., then always come back home to make seven.

Introduce the concepts of addition and subtraction with a variety of books. First, focus on addition with *Quack and count* (Baker, 2004) where children can see pictures of groups of ducks joined together with rhyming prose, such as "Splashing as they leap and dive; 7 ducklings, 2 plus 5." In the book *Ten on the sled* (Norman, 2010), ten animals start out sledding down a hill and one by one they fall off, allowing for an introduction to the concept of subtraction. Children can also see animals being added one by one to accompany Rooster, and then subtracted from the group one at a time as they leave for other adventures in *Rooster's off to see the world* (Carle, 1972).

Children can begin to learn complements of ten with the book *Ten flashing fireflies* (Sturges, 1995), where they can see pictures of fireflies in the night sky. The characters in the book catch a firefly on each page, so the reader can see one in the jar and nine in the sky, then two in the jar and eight in the sky, and so on. Children can use counters to make two piles that match the progression of the book, one and nine, two and eight, etc. When the children have practiced the complements of ten for several days, put ten counters on display then cover some counters with your hand and see if they can tell you how many you are hiding (for example, if five counters are showing, there must be five hidden under your hand).

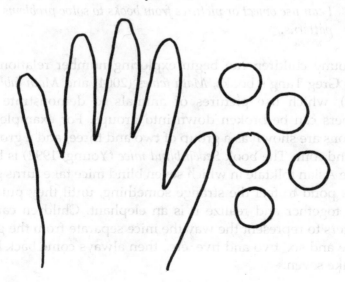

Children can start to see patterns everywhere with the books *Pattern fish* (Harris, 2000) and *Pattern bugs* (Harris, 2001). These books include rhyming text along with pictures of patterns on fish and bugs according to color, shape, and size. There are also examples of oral patterns, such as in the way the butterfly will "flutter-float, flutter-float." In the book *Beep beep, vroom vroom!* (Murphy, 2000), a child lines up toy cars using patterns based on the color of the cars. Children can use toys and other objects in the classroom to copy the patterns in the story. In the book series by Michael Dahl, children can see patterns and relationships in numbers when skip counting as they count buttons by ten in *Bunches of buttons* (2006), see pairs of footprints in *Footprints in the snow* (2005), and find five dots on insects in *Lots of ladybugs* (2004). There are several books in this series that children can use to see pictures of real-world examples of counting by twos, fives, and tens.

Connecting Patterns and Number Relationships to the Environment

Teachers can create classroom activities and centers for guided and independent practice of counting concepts to honor the active and multi-modal nature of young children's learning. By varying the types of activities each day, all children will have engaged in several activities by the end of the week. Children should explore and create patterns as well as number relationships with a variety of materials:

In the block center:

◆ Include sets of blocks that include several colors so children can create patterns with the colors or shapes, such as red, blue, red, blue or square, triangle, square, triangle.
◆ Provide toys or manipulatives (Lego, links, pattern tiles) that allow children to create and build patterns.
◆ Include a bucket of Unifix cubes and cards with patterns created with cubes for children to copy and extend.

In the dramatic play center:

◆ With the story *Five little monkeys jumping on the bed*, allow children to make a bed, add stuffed animals (monkeys) and retell the story of monkeys jumping on the bed and then falling out of the bed one by one.

◆ Place *Ten on a Sled* in your dramatic play area and add sleds and several stuffed animals. Add clothing for dressing up to play in the snow. Allow children to retell the story of falling off the sled one by one using sleds, stuffed animals, and themselves.

At the sensory table or in a sensory bin:

◆ Provide materials to build tens frames; Legos, old picture frames, post-it notes, egg cartons, chenille stems, tinker toys, popsicle sticks, long strips from bulletin board borders, cookie sheets, and tape. Children can create frames and practice filling them with a variety of classroom objects that represent two different groups, such as colored pom poms, counters, and square tiles.

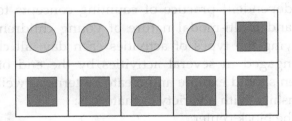

◆ Have children create shapes in sand or play dough with cookie cutters, then create or extend a pattern with the shapes.

At the art center:

◆ At the easel, set out two colors of paint and encourage children to create patterns using the two colors.

◆ Put out Bingo daubers for children to create patterns with two different colors; use the daubers to create two rows of dots to equal ten.

At the manipulative center:

◆ Provide chenille stems, beads, and a variety of buttons and pattern cards. Allow children to copy patterns; then they can match buttons to number symbols provided in the center.

◆ Children can choose a domino from a basket and fill in the dots on a blank domino on a record sheet, counting all of the dots to record the total. Include only dominoes with number on both sides (no blank sides) with sums up to ten.

◆ Create a set of 5 × 7 inch cards with stickers, putting one sticker on a card and up to nine stickers on a card (each sticker should be the same design). Children can combine two numeral cards that make ten.

At snack time:

◆ Give out crackers with two different shapes, then have the children create an AB pattern on their plate by alternating the shapes.

◆ Use ice cube trays to serve small snacks (one item per compartment) and model subtraction as each item is eaten one at a time.

Enhance the learning environment by adding the following:

◆ Have children go on a pattern hunt by searching for patterns in your environment. Look at clothing, furniture, and building structures to identify patterns inside the school and on the playground as well.

◆ Embed patterns in your classroom. Alternate shapes or colors on the floor for lining up, for nameplates or labels on cubbies, or when displaying children's work.

◆ Sing a finger play about taking away, such as five little monkeys jumping on the bed, five little pumpkins sitting on a gate, etc.

◆ Display a number line with the tens highlighted, then with the fives highlighted, then eventually with the twos highlighted; talk about the patterns in the highlighted numerals such as, all the tens have a zero.

Make intentional decisions, when setting up the learning environment, to facilitate patterning and number relationships. If children are working on ABAB patterns, select two colors, shapes, blocks, manipulatives for exploration and pattern play. Provide two colors at the paint easel, fill the sensory table with two different colored beads and chenille stems for stringing, provide two types of crackers at snack, etc. Model how you can build patterns using these binary choices. When children begin to expand patterns (ABCABC), expand given choices to three (paint colors, blocks, shapes, etc.) across the environment.

Reasoning and Proof via Exploration of Patterns and Number Relationships

Children can begin to explore the reasoning behind patterns and number relationships as well, as prove their answer is correct, by applying the following *I Can* statements:

◆ *I can share my answer using math vocabulary about patterns.*
◆ *I can listen to how my friends solve pattern and number problems.*

◆ *I can solve math problems about pattern and numbers in more than one way.*

In addition to using centers for independent practice, provide opportunities for children to work and explore concepts with a partner or as a member of a small group to enhance their reasoning skills. When children work with others they can make a pattern and have others copy or extend the pattern. Encourage them to share their answer using math vocabulary as they state the pattern aloud using letters such as AB when creating a pattern with two elements. This will help children "prove" they have created a pattern. They can also learn how their friends solved the same problem by listening when their friends state the pattern aloud. They can walk around the room together to point out and talk about patterns in the room such as in the block area or on the carpet.

Children can learn to solve problems about patterning and number relationships in more than one way. Use the situations in a literature book to explore number relationships such as complements of ten. For example, read a page of *Ten Flashing Fireflies*, cover the picture of the jar and ask, "How many fireflies are in the jar?" Show the page of the fireflies in the sky then give children ten counters and have them work to figure out how many fireflies are in the jar if there are five fireflies in the sky. Ask children to share how they found the answer so they can see there are many ways to solve a problem.

Children can share how they solved problems involving patterns by extending an AB pattern with manipulatives. Then ask how they solved the problem with probing questions such as, "How did you know the next color in the pattern would be red? Can you show me the pattern by touching the cubes when you say the letters, AB?"

Communication of Patterns and Number Relationships among Young Children

Children should practice using academic language for mathematics each day. The vocabulary related to patterns and number relationships include: *one more, one less, ten, pattern, add, subtract, next*. Young children can communicate patterning and number relationships when they apply the following *I Can* statements:

◆ *I can imitate building a pattern.*
◆ *I can find and label a pattern.*
◆ *I can use math vocabulary to describe patterns and number relationships.*

Teachers should first model the use of these vocabulary terms so children can begin to understand how they are used. For example, using the word *pattern* consistently when pointing out patterns in a story, song or in the classroom. Then encourage children to imitate the word or phrase with the word *pattern* such as stating, "When you find a pattern on the page I want you to raise your hand then say *the pattern I see is . . ."*

Children should also begin to label their drawings when appropriate. When copying a pattern, children can color in a picture of connected Unifix cubes using two colors to create an AB pattern. Then they can use the two colors to write or trace A and B below each corresponding cube.

When solving a real-world problem, children should use appropriate vocabulary to communicate their thought processes. If they are giving out a pencil to each person at their table and they need another pencil, prompt them to say, "I need *one more* pencil." As they create a discover patterns they should name the pattern by stating, "I made an AB *pattern*. It is red, blue, red, blue."

Below is a sample of areas in the classroom that can be designed to foster independent practice for exploring patterns.

Blocks	Dramatic Play	Manipulatives
Add a variety of blocks including cardboard blocks, waffle blocks, wooden blocks, and foam blocks to the area. Include examples of patterns (in a photo or drawing) for children to copy with the blocks.	Play and retell patterns in stories with dramatic play materials using books such as *Ten on a sled*, *The napping house*, *There was an old lady who swallowed a fly*.	Provide pattern cards so children can copy the pattern with the appropriate manipulatives (Unifix cubes, colored links, counting bears, buttons). Start with AB then include ABC or ABB patterns.
Easel	Sensory Table	Writing
Place two colors of paint and examples of patterns (ABAB) they can create by filling in shapes on an easel with the two colors.	Place yarn and chenille sticks at the sensory table with colored beads. Allow children to create patterns by stringing the objects onto the sticks or yarn.	Children can use their fingers to practice writing numbers, letters and symbols in salt, pudding or cornmeal. Have them create a pattern with numbers, letters or symbols.
Gross Motor	Snack	Outdoors
In a large open space, have children move in a pattern such as hop, spin, hop, spin. Play music with repetitive phrases and patterns and move to the beat.	Display two different types of fruit. Have children serve themselves two different types of fruits and make a pattern on their plate or mat.	Go on a pattern hunt around the school. How many patterns can you find on signs, in addresses or embedded in nature? Be sure to take and post photos with the patterns.

Partnering with Families and Community

Families can extend the activities and build on the concepts at home when they have examples of concepts related to patterning and number relationships. Include a list of books for patterns and number relationships appropriate for 3–5 year olds, which can be found at the local library.

Family workshops can foster book making and encourage families to create books for their children with repetitive and predictable patterns. Books can be constructed using stickers to reinforce the concept of simple addition or subtraction by adding or taking away objects on each page. For example place the appropriate number of stickers on a page and describe them as follows; "There are two balls. I will add one more and now there are three balls." Each family can select stickers of high interest and quantities that are appropriate for their child.

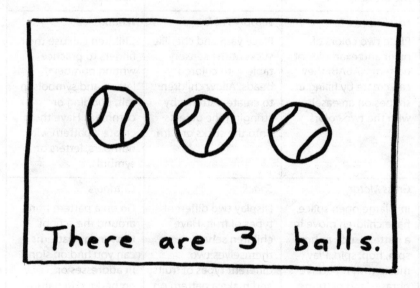

In order to practice patterns and number relationships in the community, encourage families to begin collecting small objects (sticks, leaves, rocks, pine cones). When you have ten of one type, practice moving the objects into two groups; count the objects in one group then see if the child can tell how many objects are in the other group without counting. Families can also use these materials to create patterns and reinforce vocabulary.

Below is a sample newsletter you can create for families so they can continue to practice the math concepts and skills at home. Or you can include a math section into your current family newsletter.

Weekly Newsletter

Practice these math activities with your child in daily routines outside of school.

Topic: Patterns and number relationships

Vocabulary

Vocabulary words: **one more, one less, ten, pattern, add, subtract, next**

1. Create word cards with your child. Look at the word cards and *say* the words.

2. As your child looks at the words, have him/her tell a family member what the word card says.

3. Your child will show you how to do the word card by performing an action when shown the word card. For example, have your child hold up all of their fingers when they say the word **ten**.

4. Duplicate the word cards and *play* a memory matching game.

Use these words while performing household routines such as putting out plates for each person at the table and saying when you need **one more** plate. Or make a **pattern** together with toys and ask what will come **next**.

At Home

Engage in a pattern hunt around the home. Look for repeating patterns in wallpaper, tile, clothing, dishes, curtains, and any other items in the home.

Create patterns using common objects including; two colors of plastic cups, pasta noodles, cereal, socks or buttons. Take photos of the pattern creations and send to the teacher to post in the classroom.

Use objects in the home to create groups of ten. For example, set out five spoons and ask your child to count out more spoons until there are ten. Then say, "I have five spoons and you have five spoons. Five and five more makes ten."

At Play

Count the number of blocks used to build a structure or the number of toys such as cars or dolls lined up in a row. Then add one more, saying the number aloud each time.

Create a pattern with the toys such as red block, blue block, red block, blue block. Have your child copy your pattern and add on to your pattern, asking which color block would come next.

On the Go

While traveling, search for patterns in the environment and in nature. It could be patterns in fences and flowerbeds, on signs or buildings.

Books about patterns and number relationships to check out at the library:

Ten flashing fireflies—Sturges
Rooster's off to see the world—Carle
Beep beep, vroom vroom!—Murphy
Bunches of buttons—Dahl

Looking Ahead

The learning activities in this chapter can strengthen young children's skills with patterns and number relationships. These skills can be defined as learning targets. Learning targets should be posted in your classroom for children and visitors to be made aware of the learning that is taking place. The targets should be shared with families to reinforce their understanding of learning activities in the classroom and those sent home for practice.

The following *I Can* statements are suggestions for learning targets and should be tailored to your children's abilities:

- ◆ *I can find patterns at home and school.*
- ◆ *I can find patterns in numbers.*
- ◆ *I can make ten with objects.*
- ◆ *I can add to a group of objects.*
- ◆ *I can take away from a group of objects.*

4

Establishing Problem-Solving Routines to Promote Measurement

Young children begin to make sense of their world by creating categories—animals are compared to their pet dog, people are grouped as either children or adults, and toys get put away based on size or type. The concept of measurement includes making comparisons and occurs during real-life events such as when children notice their brother is taller than their friend. At play, children put objects in order such as placing toy dinosaurs side by side from smallest to biggest. Children also "measure" toys and other objects using non-standard units such as blocks or when they measure their own height next to a piece of furniture.

Additionally, young children are noticing the concept of time as it relates to their immediate environment such as asking, "When will we get there?" while in the car or "When do we have snack?" while at school. Learning the order of events at school or the steps of a task at home, as well as making predictions about what will happen next, can lead to independent completion of these tasks.

Finally, young children can begin each day by answering a question with a binary choice such as a yes or no. The questions can be related to their home life such as "Do you have a pet?" or "Do you like chicken nuggets?" Children can use a Post-it note with their name on it to indicate their choice of yes or no. The yes and no columns would start at the same baseline so children could see which column is taller to represent the most responses.

The following skills will be included in this chapter:

◆ compare two objects in relation to each other;
◆ put three objects in order (shortest to tallest, shortest to longest, etc.);
◆ sort and describe objects according to attributes such as color or size;
◆ measure items with non-standard units (blocks, string);
◆ learn and predict the schedule at school and home;
◆ reply and record responses to yes or no questions.

Problem Solving with Measurement

Set up scenarios for children to help solve a problem such as choosing the size of objects needed for a task, predicting the sequence of a task, and sorting objects before putting them away. Teachers should provide opportunities for children to solve problems that arise in the context of the classroom routines and the typical school day using the following *I Can* statements:

◆ *I can discover how to measure an object.*
◆ *I can use words and pictures to solve a measurement problem.*
◆ *I can show others how I solved a problem using measurement.*

Children can be exposed to measuring the length of familiar objects such as shoes or boots. They can use Unifix cubes, lined up end to end, to measure a crayon. They can report how many cubes long for the crayon and then look for other objects that are the same length. They can find other objects in the classroom such as markers and paint brushes and use cubes to measure each of those objects. Create opportunities for children to use pictures to solve a problem such as comparing two or three objects. Children can trace the objects on paper, lining them up at the bottom of their paper, to show how they solved the problem of putting them in order from shortest to longest. Encourage children to talk about their picture so they can practice using math words such as *short/shorter, long/longer*, and *tall/taller*. Use a children's literature book or situation in the classroom to create a math problem involving measurement. For example, when putting away materials and toys in the classroom, tell the children you want to put away the big items first to make sure there is enough room for them, then you will put away the smaller items. The children can work with a friend to find a big item and bring it to the center of the classroom. Then work as a class to find which of those items is the biggest and put them away from biggest to smallest (Weston, 1993).

Representing Measurement with Literacy

Teachers can provide experiences with books that allow for demonstrating various concepts of measurement such as sorting and comparing. The use of children's literature can facilitate the application of the following *I Can* statements:

- ◆ *I can use real objects to solve measurement problems.*
- ◆ *I can use pictures of objects to solve measurement problems.*
- ◆ *I can begin to use symbols to solve measurement problems.*

There are several books with colorful illustrations showing children how to sort familiar objects according to specific attributes. The story *The button box* (Reid, 1990) is about a boy who loves to play with his grandma's large collection of buttons. The word *sort* is introduced early in the story and each page shows how the boy puts them into categories such as sparkly buttons, cloth-covered buttons, metal, wooden and leather buttons, and shiny buttons from uniforms. Children can sift through a jar of buttons in the classroom and use small containers to sort buttons into categories.

Children can see how another child categorizes objects in the story *Sam sorts* (Jocelyn, 2017). As Sam is putting away his toys he counts objects that are alike, puts the round objects in a pile and gathers up all of his rocks together. Children can use the same strategy when cleaning up the classroom as they count similar objects and put objects together by color, type, or size.

Hannah's collections (Jocelyn, 2004) is an example of how to use collections of objects for a show and tell activity. Hannah's teacher asks students to bring one of their collections to school but Hannah has many collections from which to choose. The collage-style illustrations show how she sorts and counts her collections of buttons, shells, feathers and more.

Use familiar stories to practice comparing objects such as *Goldilocks and the three bears* (Brett, 1996). Children can act out the story while they put the objects and animals in order from smallest to biggest. Another story that children can use to put animals in order is *The three billy goats gruff* (Pinkney, 2017). Children can draw the billy goats to show their size and practice their math vocabulary to retell the story of the three goats that get bigger as they meet the troll. Read *How long is a whale?* (Limentani, 2017) for children to explore the concepts of length and size as the illustrations compare sizes of various underwater creatures. Introduce the concept of weight with the book *How much does a ladybug weigh?* (Limentani, 2016). Each common animal and insect is compared to each other in a countdown from one to ten: "10 ants = 1 ladybug, 9 ladybugs = 1 grasshopper," and so on. Use a balance scale to put one object, such as a toy horse, on one side then see how many teddy bear counters are equal to the horse. Create a class book to represent all of the comparisons.

One of the best books for explaining the concept of time to young children is *A second is a hiccup: A child's book of time* (Hutchins, 2007). Children can relate to a second as a hiccup, a minute as 60 hiccups or 60 hops, an hour as the time to walk to the park, play and return home. Young children can talk about things that have happened or will happen, but they cannot yet understand or talk about these event in terms of units of time (days, weeks) or sequence (Beneke, Ostrosky, & Katz, 2008). Instead of using a traditional calendar, use Post-It notes, photographs or drawings to display the schedule for the day or at the end of the morning and afternoon class, review an event that occurred. Linear representations help young children conceptualize a day as a unit of time and provide opportunities to emphasize time-related vocabulary (before, after, later, earlier) as children add a new activity, review or anticipate the day's events.

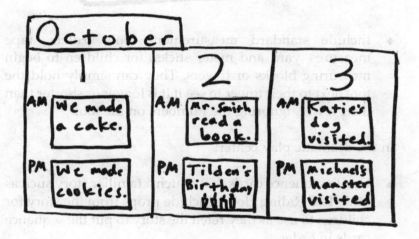

Connecting Measurement to the Environment

Teachers can create classroom activities and centers for guided and independent practice of measurement concepts to honor the active and multi-modal nature of young children's learning. By varying the types of activities each day, all children will have engaged in several activities by the end of the week. Children should explore measurement concepts with a variety of materials:

In the block center:

◆ Include sets of blocks that include several sizes so children can compare the sizes as well as build towers of different heights.

◆ Provide non-standard measurement tools (Lego, links, Unifix cubes) children can manipulate by placing end to end to informally measure the length of objects.

◆ Include standard measurement tools (rulers, tape measures, yard and meter sticks) for children to begin measuring blocks or towers. They can simply hold the tool next to their tower to see if it is longer or shorter than their tower, ignoring the numbers on the tool.

In the dramatic play center:

◆ Create sequence cards that match a familiar story such as Little Red Riding Hood. Include props from the story for children to use as they retell the story to put the sequence cards in order.
◆ Place the book *Goldilocks and the three bears* in your dramatic play area and add cardboard representations or stuffed toys to represent Goldilocks and the baby, mama and papa bear. Add kitchen and household items to allow children to retell the story of Goldilocks finding the different-sized chairs, bowls and beds.
◆ Provide various kitchen gadgets that nest such as bowls, measuring cups and spoons for children to use as they pretend they are cooking.

At the sensory table or in a sensory bin:

◆ Provide materials with different textures for children to sort and classify: Lego, chenille stems, Tinker Toys, colored craft sticks, pom-poms, buttons, feathers, shells, etc. Children can use muffin tins to sort items such as all of the red items, all of the shells or all of the round items.

◆ Have children create towers in sand that gradually get taller using different-sized cups as the molds for the towers; children can roll out play dough "snakes" and put them in order from shortest to tallest.

At the art center:

◆ At the easel, set out one color of paint each day along with blackline drawings of objects that represent that color for children to fill in.

◆ Have children paint people in their family and then talk about which one is taller/shorter than they are.

At the manipulative center:

◆ Provide string of different lengths along with various objects from the classroom for children to "measure" by finding objects shorter than the string and objects longer than the string.

◆ Put out a tray of buttons and sorting cards so children can sort the buttons according to the attribute on the card such as all of the red buttons, all of the shiny buttons, or all of the buttons with fabric.

At snack time:

◆ Give out crackers with two or three different colors then have children sort the crackers on their plate by putting them into piles based on color.

◆ Cut food such as carrots into various lengths and have children put them in order on their plate from shortest to longest.

Enhance the learning environment by adding the following:

◆ Have children go on a size hunt and find the tallest object in the room, the biggest object, and the shortest object. Then do the same in other parts of the school as well as in the area around the school.

◆ Sort objects when cleaning up the classroom by putting all of the blocks in a container, all of the cubes in another container, etc.

◆ Act out the stories of *Goldilocks and the three bears* and *The three billy goats gruff* using cardboard bears and goats for children to hold as each sized bear or goat is introduced in the story.

◆ Display the agenda for the day with sentence strips using both a word and picture; talk about the events and what will come next; take away the sentence strip when the event is completed.

◆ Have children predict what they will do next based on their experience in a typical school day. Ask questions such as, "It is time to wash our hands for snack so what will we do first?"

Below is a sample of areas in the classroom that can be designed to foster independent practice for children to sort objects according to specific attributes such as color, shape or size.

Reasoning and Proof via Exploration of Measurement

Children can begin to explore the reasoning behind measurement concepts, as well as prove their answer is correct, by applying the following *I Can* statements:

◆ *I can share my answer using measurement vocabulary words.*
◆ *I can listen to how my friends measured the same object.*
◆ *I can measure objects in more than one way.*

Blocks	Dramatic Play	Manipulatives
Add a variety of blocks to the area (Lego, wooden and cardboard blocks, etc.). Have children sort the blocks into bins by color, size or shape.	Using the book *Sam sorts*, put toys from the story and hula hoops for children to sort according to size, color or type.	Provide a large bin of Unifix cubes and small trays for children to sort the cubes by color. Encourage children to connect cubes then compare lengths.
Easel	Sensory Table	Writing
Place a different color of paint and pictures of objects that represent that color in the art center each day.	Place a variety of buttons, beads or small fabric swatches at the sensory table with a muffin pan for sorting.	Provide envelopes, papers, writing tools and the names of the children. Allow the children to create, sort and deliver mail to their peers.
Gross Motor	Snack	Outdoors
Place a variety of sizes of balls in a bin and hoops on the ground for children to explore and sort by type.	Display a variety of crackers for children to sort by color, shape or size.	Look for objects that have a common attribute such as round objects, metal objects or green objects.

Encourage children to use measurement words as they talk about an item they brought in, such as an apple. Have all of the children at a table put their apple in front of them and see who can use the words *smaller* and *bigger* to describe some of the apples. Then they can use cubes to measure the height of the apples at their table using the words *taller* and *shorter*. With a balance scale they can select two apples, putting one on each side of the balance scale, then use the words *heavier* and *lighter* to describe the apples.

Have children work with a partner to select an object in the classroom to measure. Provide them with a variety of small materials such as cubes, links, and square tiles. Allow each child to choose one of the materials to measure the length of the object by putting the small materials end to end. Have children compare how they measured the same object with different materials.

Have the children choose an object in the classroom such as a computer or table to be measured. Measure the length of the object with small materials, such as square inch tiles, and record the number of tiles for the length of the object. Then choose a larger material, such as wooden rectangular blocks, and record the number of blocks for the length of the object. Talk about how fewer blocks were used because they are longer than the tiles.

Communication of Measurement among Young Children

Children should practice using academic language for mathematics each day. The vocabulary related to measurement includes: *small/smaller, big/bigger, short/shorter, long/longer, tall/taller, heavy/heavier, light/lighter, measure, same, sort, time, next, first, last, predict.* Young children can communicate about measurement when they apply the following *I Can* statements:

◆ *I can imitate measuring objects.*
◆ *I can use drawings to show measurement.*
◆ *I can use measurement vocabulary to solve a problem.*

Model using measurement words and materials so children can imitate you and learn how to eventually measure on their own. Tell the children, "I am going to see how many links are the *same* as this name tag. To *measure* the name tag, I have to put the links across the name tag and count how many links there are." Then have the children repeat the process with the links and their name tag. The children should show a friend how they measured the name tag using the same vocabulary terms you used.

As children learn sequencing of events, have them draw a routine from the school day, such as getting ready to go outside, eating snack, or cleaning up toys. Then have them tell you about their picture using the terms *first, next,* and *last.* Have adults in the classroom record what each child said on a piece of paper and attach it to their drawings.

Refer back to the name tag measurement activity and tell children they are to find objects in the classroom that are *shorter* than their name tag. Have them use their links and, with a friend, go on a hunt for objects that are shorter than their name tag. Then tell them to look for objects that are *longer* than their name tag. Each pair of children should find at least one object that is shorter and one object that is longer and be able to tell you about the objects using the appropriate vocabulary.

Partnering with Families and Community

Families can extend the activities and build on the concepts at home when they have examples of concepts and vocabulary involved with measurement, such as sorting, comparing, and sequencing. They should also be aware of the types of activities that can be completed within and outside of the home. Include a list of books with various measurement topics appropriate for 3–5 year olds which can be found at the local library.

Plan a family workshop at your school site with activities related to measurement so families can see how the children are learning these concepts in the classroom. Put out different types of objects and toys they might have at home, then engage in activities for sorting and comparing. Have families create activity cards on 3 × 3 pieces of tagboard (using stick figures and simple drawings) depicting household routines involving several steps, such as washing dishes, doing laundry, or making a bed. Talk about how these cards can be used for sequencing activities along with the vocabulary words *first, next, last.*

Partner with a local YMCA or park district to set up a community-based learning event for concepts related to measurement. Use a gym or other large open space to set out various sports and fitness equipment. Talk about and demonstrate how each piece of equipment is used, then encourage children to use vocabulary words such as *small/smaller, big/bigger, short/shorter, long/longer, tall/taller, heavy/heavier, light/lighter* to describe the equipment. Have families work together to sort the equipment by attributes such as color, size, shape, or sport. Put out large hula hoops that can be used to hold the different groups of equipment. As a culminating activity, choose two attributes, such as round and brown, and put the corresponding equipment into the two hula hoops. Then use the hula hoops as a Venn Diagram and challenge the children to find equipment that can be part of both groups, such as a basketball, and put those into the overlapping section.

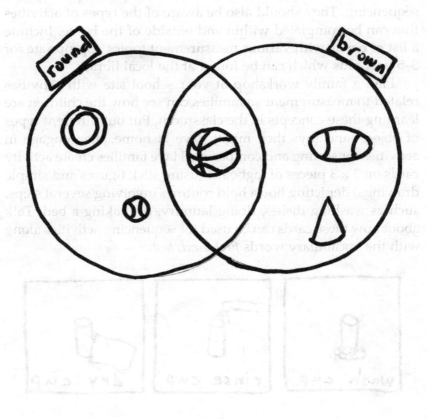

Below is a sample newsletter you can create for families so they can continue to practice the math concepts and skills at home. Or you can include a math section into your current family newsletter.

Weekly Newsletter

Practice these math activities with your child in daily routines outside of school.

Topic: Measurement

Vocabulary

Vocabulary words: **small/smaller, big/bigger, short/shorter, long/longer, tall/taller, heavy/heavier, light/lighter, measure, same, sort** (to group items that are similar), **time, first, next, last, predict** (use information to figure out what will happen)

1. Create word cards with your child. Look at the word cards and *say* the words.

2. As your child looks at the words, have him/her *tell* a family member what the word card says.

3. Your child will show you how to *do* the word card by performing an action when shown the word card. For example, have your child find two items and then stretch out their hands to show you which one is **longer**.

4. Duplicate the word cards and *play* a memory matching game.

Use these words throughout the day when performing household routines, such as doing laundry or setting the table. Talk about what you should do **first**, what steps come **next**, and what you should do **last**.

At Home

Compare objects by length, height, and weight by looking in different areas of the home to find the tallest, smallest, lightest, or longest item. Using a ruler, find objects shorter than the ruler and objects longer than the ruler (do not worry about the numbers on the ruler).

Sort objects while doing household chores. Talk about where to put dishes, such as glasses on one shelf and plates on another. Put clothes in piles according to type, such as a pile of socks, a pile of shorts, and a pile of pants.

Talk about the time of day and order of daily routines, such as eating breakfast or lunch, leaving for school, walking the dog, and getting ready for bed.

Create a daily question on a dry erase board or mini chalkboard to which your child can answer yes or no, such as: Do you want pizza for dinner? Did you like it when we went to the new park yesterday? Involve other family members and use tally marks or their name to indicate their preference.

At Play

Sort toys by color. Put all of the red items together, then blue items, etc. Then choose another way to *sort* them, such as vehicles in one group and stuffed animals in another group.

Put a group of toys in order from smallest to biggest and then from shortest to tallest.

Use dolls or other figures to act out a favorite story using the words *first*, *next*, and *last*.

As you read a story to your child, have him or her *predict* what will happen next. You can also ask your child yes or no questions about what just happened in the story.

On the Go

While traveling, look for objects of various length, such as trucks and cars on the road; look for buildings of various heights around the community. Use the vocabulary words as you point out the vehicles and buildings.

Have your child predict what time you will arrive at a destination and watch the clock while you are traveling to see how close he/she can get to the actual time. Talk about how long the trip lasts so your child can begin to understand the concept of time.

Books about measurement to check out at the library:

Sam sorts—Jocelyn
Goldilocks and the three bears—Brett
How long is a whale?—Limentani
A second is a hiccup—Hutchins

Looking Ahead

The learning activities in this chapter can strengthen young children's skills with measurement concepts. These skills can be defined as learning targets. Learning targets should be posted in your classroom for children and visitors to be made aware of the learning that is taking place. The targets should be shared with families to reinforce their understanding of learning activities in the classroom.

The following *I Can* statements are suggestions for learning targets and should be tailored to your children' abilities:

- ◆ *I can measure objects in the classroom and at home.*
- ◆ *I can compare objects.*
- ◆ *I can learn my schedule at school and home.*
- ◆ *I can predict what happens next in my schedule.*
- ◆ *I can answer yes or no questions.*

5

Establishing Problem-Solving Routines to Promote Concepts of Geometry

Young children are surrounded by mathematical environments filled with geometric concepts. They discover circles on garbage trucks, rectangles on cereal boxes, and squares lining the sidewalks, which represent the earliest understandings of shapes and space. As young children continue to explore materials in their environment, they are seen drawing shapes, building with blocks, and rotating or flipping puzzle pieces.

As young children interact with objects in their environment, they notice similarities and differences. They may notice a ball and a plate are both round but only the ball can roll. They also become aware of spatial relationships and use vocabulary such as *in*, *out*, and *above* to respond to and describe the location of people, objects, and animals. These daily experiences are packed with mathematical concepts that fascinate and challenge young thinkers and can eventually prompt analytical thought, growing precision, and abstraction.

The following geometry skills are included in this chapter:

◆ recognize, name, and match two-dimensional shapes;
◆ recognize, name, and match three-dimensional shapes;
◆ use appropriate vocabulary to describe position;
◆ sort collections of shapes by type;
◆ combine two-dimensional shapes to create new shapes;
◆ name the face of a three-dimensional object;
◆ describe shapes by their attributes.

Problem Solving with Geometry

Teachers should provide opportunities for children to solve problems about shapes that arise in the context of classroom routines and the typical school day. Use the following *I Can* statements as children solve problems about shapes in space:

◆ *I can name different shapes.*
◆ *I can describe shapes.*
◆ *I can name shapes when describing pictures and objects.*

In order to make sense of and problem solve using geometry, young children are expected to begin naming shapes using mathematical vocabulary: *squares, circles, triangles, rectangles, hexagons, cubes, cones, cylinders, and spheres*. Children gradually become exposed to these shapes in various sizes, colors, and orientations as part of their environments. Once young children begin to recognize these shapes, teachers need to encourage the use of the correct vocabulary and description of the position of shapes relative to other shapes and objects. Some appropriate vocabulary for young children to use when describing relative position is *above, below, beside, in front of, behind*, and *next to*.

Problem-solving skills evolve as young children begin to notice differences between two-dimensional, "flat" shapes (square, circle, triangle, rectangle, hexagon) and three-dimensional, "fat" shapes (cube, cone, cylinder, sphere). They begin describing similarities and differences when comparing the size of shapes and may even discover the different number of sides comprising a rectangle and a triangle. Teachers need to create opportunities for young children to compare specific two-dimensional and three-dimensional shapes, such as a paper circle and a ball. They can use mathematical vocabulary to explain that they are both round, but the ball is a sphere and can roll.

Young children first use objects, illustrations, and photos to practice naming shapes. Next, they copy shapes found in their environment by drawing and tracing two-dimensional shapes or using play dough and toothpicks to create three-dimensional shapes. Once they are familiar with these shapes, they are ready to build composite shapes by putting shapes together. Young children may do this when playing with different-shaped blocks, when they put a triangle on top of a square to represent a house. Young children can also create larger shapes using smaller shapes, such as putting two small square tiles together to make one large rectangle. As they compose shapes, be sure to name the shapes they are creating. When they compose their shapes and take their shapes apart or decompose them, be sure to use this mathematical vocabulary to describe their actions.

Representing Geometry with Literacy

The following *I Can* statements are reinforced with the use of children's literature.

- ◆ *I can use real objects to explore different shapes.*
- ◆ *I can use pictures of shapes to solve problems.*
- ◆ *I can listen to how my friends find and name shapes in books.*

Another method of representation that promotes problem solving is the use of children's literature. Tana Hoban's *Shapes, shapes, shapes* (1986) is filled with photographs of everyday objects including houses, bridges, and food which represent circles, squares, triangles, and rectangles. This literature could serve as an introduction to a week-long shape hunt. Post pictures of each shape around the room near the item (a circle near the clock, a rectangle near the window) and have children hunt for each shape. Young children can work in pairs. One child can hold a clipboard with outlines of each shape while the other child uses pointers to locate the shapes.

A book reinforcing attributes of shapes is Marcie Aboff's *If you were a triangle* (2009). The characters use triangles in the environment, including triangle instruments and slices of watermelon. On the left side of each two-page spread, a sentence begins with "If you were a triangle . . . ." The terms used in the book can be used to describe attributes of triangles, as well as pyramids, such as *side, face, corners, angles, straight, flat,* and *length*, with pictures and examples for support. There are also illustrations of composite shapes, such as two isosceles right triangles of the same size formed to make a square. Provide a pile of triangles for each child that varies in color, size, and type. As you read the story, children can hold up the matching triangles. Later, they can use their triangles for sorting and making composite shapes.

Reading literature not written specifically for mathematics supports integration of other content areas with geometry. *Home* (2015) by Carson Ellis gives children opportunities to explore different types of homes using their knowledge of shapes, combining geometry with social science. Illustrations depict homes of animals, homes from nursery rhymes, and homes from across the world. The book provides a limitless opportunity to label windows, rooftops, doors, smoke stacks, turrets, and tree houses using shapes and positional concepts, reinforcing the different places people call home. *Last stop on Market Street* (2015) by Matt de la Peña reinforces shapes and spatial concepts as the characters ride the bus across a bustling city. The illustrations provide opportunities to search for familiar shapes and positional concepts to discuss, including *beside*, *in front of*, and *next to*. Both selections help children make connections and see shapes in their own homes and communities.

Connecting Geometry to the Environment

In addition to literature connections, classroom centers provide independent and guided practice of geometry concepts while honoring the active and multi-modal nature of young children's learning. Using objects found in the classroom, such as wooden blocks, inch tiles, or objects from home, such as empty cereal boxes and cans, help children make connections between home, school, shapes, and space.

Intentional planning of center activities allows children to practice their understanding of geometry concepts. Design your environment with centers and create a rotation schedule so, by the end of a defined period of time, all children have engaged in several activities representing each concept in the geometry domain. Include independent practice that allows young children to explore shapes and spatial relationships across their environment:

In the block center:

◆ Bring in three-dimensional shapes, such as cans, cartons, boxes, paper towel rolls, etc. Allow children to build structures with the solid shapes and take pictures of each one. Display the pictures on your classroom website or print them out and display them. Children can count and name the shapes used in their structures.

- ◆ Convert the block area into a construction site. Display blueprints and label both two-dimensional and three-dimensional shapes on buildings or blocks.
- ◆ Use Magna-tiles or pool noodles to build and reinforce the names of shapes.
- ◆ Create an obstacle course with pool noodles and move over, under, and through the shapes.

In the dramatic play center:

- ◆ Convert the dramatic play area into a store. Collect and display three-dimensional shapes (boxes and cans) as merchandise for sorting. Add signage with numbers for store items.
- ◆ Set up a pond with fishing poles (large plastic pool or sensory tub) and have children fish for paper shapes. Sort and classify shapes when the pond is empty.

At the sensory table or in a sensory bin:

- ◆ Fill the sensory table with tissue paper shapes, add tweezers, and have the children pick them up and sort the shapes into containers.
- ◆ Bury Pattern Blocks under sand in the sensory table. Have children dig, discover, and sort the shapes.
- ◆ Fill the sensory table with cylinders (drinking straws, Velcro hair rollers, water bottles, paper towel rolls, cans) for stacking, rolling, and sorting.
- ◆ Fill the sensory table with a variety of materials, such as toothpicks, chenille stems, wiffle balls, pool noodles, straws, and craft sticks. Instruct children to create each two-dimensional shape with the materials. When they are ready to create three-dimensional shapes, add play dough or clay to stick materials together.
- ◆ Provide sensory materials (salt, sand, gravel) on flat trays and allow children to use their fingers to draw shapes on the trays.

At the art center:

◆ Display wooden solid shapes, as well as household containers such as cans and cups. Children can make prints with the faces of these solids by dipping them in paint. They should be able to identify each two-dimensional shape they trace that makes up the faces of the solid shapes.

◆ Provide pattern cards or templates with the shapes outlined so children can practice putting pieces together to compose new shapes and figures.

◆ Cut apart small boxes on the seams so they can be folded and unfolded. Children can discover that a box is made up of six rectangles.

◆ Provide tissue paper shapes and clear contact paper on a window or light source. Have children compose larger shapes by placing smaller shapes together.

At the manipulative center:

◆ Provide Geoboards and rubber bands with some sample shapes and designs on dot paper. Encourage children to make as many different triangles as they can with regard to size, type, and orientation. See if they can do the same with rectangles, squares, and hexagons.

◆ Spread out a variety of Pattern Blocks and construct new shapes.

◆ Cover a hexagon piece with other shapes, such as two trapezoids or six triangles.

◆ Stamp Pattern Blocks into play dough, name the shapes, and compare the attributes, such as the number of sides.

◆ Provide paper shape pieces and encourage children to push two shapes together to form other shapes.

At the snack center:

◆ Serve snacks that represent two-dimensional or three-dimensional shapes: crackers, Cheerios, Bugles, marshmallows, cheese cubes, and donut holes.

◆ Make pizzas at snack time using pita bread or muffins cut into circles, rectangles, or triangles.

Enhance the learning environment by adding the following:

◆ Use masking tape to create shapes on the floor, carpet, or playground. Children can walk on the tape or be directed to move in and around the shapes. Provide instructions, such as "jump into the circle."
◆ Tape a series of shapes, on the floor, close to the classroom door and ask the children to line up by standing on a shape: "Stand inside the circle. Stand on the triangle."
◆ Have children "drive" cars on the shapes as roads. The same thing can be done outside on the playground with paint or chalk. Then allow the children to ride bikes, adapted equipment, or vehicles on and around the shapes.

See p. 75 for a sample of areas in the classroom that can be designed to foster independent practice for naming shapes.

Reasoning and Proof via Exploration of Geometry

Children can begin to explore the reasoning behind geometry concepts, as well as prove their answer is correct, by applying the following *I Can* statements:

◆ *I can use math vocabulary when solving problems during work and play.*
◆ *I can listen to my friends solving problems using shape vocabulary.*
◆ *I can solve problems about shapes in more than one way.*

In addition to using centers for independent practice, set up rotations that allow children to work and play together with a partner to practice reasoning skills. Encourage young children to talk about their reasoning and proof during play, providing

Blocks	Dramatic Play— Construction Site	Manipulatives
Add a variety of building materials including Magna-tiles, Lego, and cardboard bricks. Practice naming shapes while composing and decomposing using all types of blocks.	Collect boxes and cylinders for construction. Add plastic hard hats and tools. Use painter's tape to outline a building on the wall or floor and fill it in with blocks. Add photos of actual buildings for children to replicate.	Add Pattern Blocks and pattern cards for children to replicate. Be sure to name the shapes while copying the patterns— "square, triangle, square, triangle . . ."
Easel Use the face of cans, boxes, blocks, and paper towel rolls to create two-dimensional shape prints. Cut sponges into shapes and use the sponges for painting. Children should name shapes while printing.	**Sensory Table** Add clothespins, drinking straws, chenille stems, craft sticks, and play dough for constructing three-dimensional shapes. Children should name the constructed shapes.	**Writing** Add different-shaped papers for writing or scribbling letters or messages. Add blueprints and allow children to hunt for shapes on the prints. Be sure to label the shapes that are located.
Gross Motor Cut shapes from contact paper and stick them on the floor for line up or create a path using hula hoops. Have the children name the shapes while they move from one to another.	**Snack** Serve different-shaped snacks: banana slices, crackers, cheese; cut sandwiches into shapes; use cookie cutters to cut shapes into soft sliced bread. Have children request their snack by naming the shape.	**Outdoors** Draw large shapes on the playground and use them as roads for "driving." Have the children name the shapes on each road.

practice of explanation and mathematical discourse. Young children can also practice their social skills, including turn-taking and sharing materials, as they play side-by-side with their peers. Together, they can share the reasons for their decisions or choices during play.

Set up opportunities for children to solve problems involving shapes and space that require reasoning and proof. For example, tell the class you are going to rearrange the classroom and move some furniture, such as tables, easels, or storage bins, to a new location. Have children use math vocabulary related to shapes and space to describe each item and where you moved it, such as: "The table is a rectangle. It is next to the desk. The bin is a cube. It is below the window." Then have them talk about how they will have to move through the classroom with the new arrangement using vocabulary related to spatial relationships, such as: "I will walk around the table when I line up. I can sit next to the bin."

Communication of Geometry among Young Children

Children should practice using academic language for mathematics each day. The vocabulary for geometry includes words related to spatial relationships: *above, below, beside, in front of, behind,* and *next to*; and words related to shapes: *squares, circles, triangles, rectangles, hexagons, cubes, cones, cylinders,* and *spheres*. Young children can communicate about geometry when they apply the following *I Can* statements:

- ◆ *I can use positional words to describe the location of shapes.*
- ◆ *I can name two-dimensional and three-dimensional shapes.*
- ◆ *I can use shape vocabulary to describe two-dimensional and three-dimensional shapes.*

Use listening and speaking skills to reinforce geometric thinking. Increase understanding of spatial orientations by emphasizing one word or phrase, in English and home languages, for a few days each week. Model use of the word or phrase throughout the day in settings such as the classroom, hallway, and playground: "Juan is sitting *beside* his friend. We are walking *beside* the school."

Once children are familiar with two-dimensional and three-dimensional shapes as well as the spatial vocabulary, begin to use them together. For example, "The clock is a *circle*. It is *above* the door which is a *rectangle*." Then create a class book authored by children and their families, using photos or drawings of shapes found at school and home. Have children dictate descriptions of different photos or drawings using positional words to describe them. Share the book with the class and families.

Add new geometry vocabulary (square, circle, triangle, rectangle, hexagon, cone, cylinder, cube, sphere) to the word wall and send the list of words and examples home for families. Practice using these words with the children over several days to teach the meaning of the vocabulary using the *Say-Tell-Do-Play* strategy created by the Southwest Institute for Families & Children (www.swifamilies.org). On day one, show the children a word card with an illustration and printed word for each vocabulary word. Read the word and have the children repeat the words as you *say* each word. On day two, use the same word cards but, when you show each card, ask the children to *tell* a friend what each word says. On the third day, create a physical response and *do* each word. For example, use your finger to write a square in the air, hold your arms out in front of your body to form a sphere, etc. On the fourth day, create simple opportunities to *play* with the words. The playful practice can include playing a memory game, burying word cards in the sensory table, or using play dough to make the shapes. Be sure to present the word cards during play.

Encourage children to learn the words in their home language. Create posters or anchor charts of the geometric vocabulary in the various languages and post them around your environment as labels next to the corresponding shapes.

During large group activities, use songs, poems, and chants about shapes. Print the songs, poems, and chants to promote emergent literacy and lead the children in singing and chanting.

◆ Write the following on chart paper with drawings and examples of the two-dimensional and three-dimensional shapes included in the poem:

- *3D Shapes.*
- *3D shapes are fat not flat.*
- *A cone is like a party hat.*
- *A sphere is like a bouncing ball.*
- *A prism is like a building tall.*
- *A cylinder is like a can of pop.*
- *A cube is like the dice you drop.*
- *3D shapes are here and there. 3D shapes are everywhere.*

(3D Shapes, 2015)

◆ Put two-dimensional and three-dimensional shapes in a basket between two children so they can play *Shape Hide and Seek*. One child hides a shape behind his back while the other child asks questions about the attributes of the shape to guess which shape is hidden. They might ask,

"Does the shape have four sides? Are all of the sides the same length?"

Partnering with Families and Community

Families can extend the activities and build on the geometric concepts at home when they have a list of the two-dimensional and three-dimensional shapes, spatial relationship words, and attributes, along with definitions and examples. Families should also be aware of the types of activities they can replicate with resources found in the home. Share a list of books connected to geometry. Most importantly, families should be encouraged to facilitate learning about geometry by using geometric vocabulary and concepts.

Creating workshops with families helps to highlight their interests and skills, as well as introduce and reinforce vocabulary related to geometry. For example, if families have a passion for woodworking, they may facilitate a workshop to construct a simple birdhouse or bird feeder using squares, or a simple step stool using rectangles. Another families' interest in gardening may provide opportunities to teach about designing a plot for a flower or vegetable garden, reinforcing mathematical vocabulary including shapes and spatial relationships.

Partnering with community recreation centers can provide opportunities for a family motor morning where two-dimensional and three-dimensional shapes and concepts are defined and reinforced. For example, a ball is a sphere and a hula hoop is a circle. Hula hoops, a variety of balls, and different-shaped mats can be used to create an obstacle course, while reinforcing shape naming and motor exploration. Use tape to create shape paths to follow on foot or with riding toys. These simple motor activities can be replicated in the home.

Below is a sample newsletter you can create for families so they can continue to practice the math concepts and skills at home. Or you can include a math section into your current family newsletter.

Weekly Newsletter

Practice these math activities with your child in daily routines outside of school.

Topic: Geometry

Vocabulary

Vocabulary words for shapes: **square, circle, triangle, rectangle, hexagon** (six straight sides and angles), **cone, cylinder** (can-shaped solid figure), **sphere** (ball-shaped figure), **cube** (box-shaped with square on each side).

Vocabulary words for spatial relationships (position words): **next to, behind, beside, above, below, in front of**.

1. Create word cards with your child. Look at the word cards and *say* the words with your child.

2. As your child looks at the words, have him/her *tell* a family member what the word card says.

3. Your child will show you how to *do* the word card by performing a simple physical response when shown the word card. For example, when shown **circle**, use your index finger and draw a circle in the air.

4. Duplicate the word cards and *play* a memory matching game.

Use directions involving relative position words throughout the child's day. Reinforce these words during play by asking questions, such as: "Are you crawling **next to** the chair? Did you sleep **beside** your teddy bear?"

At Home

Go on a Shape Hunt in and around your home—look for things shaped like a *circle, square, triangle,* and *rectangle.* These can be furniture, food, and patterns on clothing or objects in nature.

Identify shapes that are on the table during mealtime. For example, the plate is a circle. The napkin is a square. The placemat is a rectangle.

Make sandwiches and cut them into rectangles, squares, and triangles.

At Play

Build structures using three-dimensional shapes such as building blocks, shoeboxes, cereal boxes, paper towel rolls, etc.

Use play dough to create a variety of shapes.

Take pictures of your creations and email them to school. We will print and post them in our classroom.

Play *Simon Says* using position words. "Simon Says, put your hands *behind* your back. Simon Says, put a toy *above* your head."

On the Go

Ask families to take pictures of the shapes in their homes or communities. Ask them to email the photos to school, then print them for a class book or display to exemplify the compilation of shapes and families in your learning environment.

While traveling, search for shapes in your neighborhood. Look at the shapes on buildings, on signage, or in the park. Can you find a rectangle (door)? Can you spot a triangle (traffic sign)? Do you see squares (windows)? Ask children to name the shape in their home language.

Books about shapes to check out at the library:

Last stop on Market Street—de la Peña
If you were a triangle—Aboff
Shapes, shapes, shapes—Hoban
Mouse shapes—Walsh

Looking Ahead

The learning activities in this chapter can strengthen young children's geometry skills. These skills can be defined as learning targets. Learning targets should be posted in your classroom for children and visitors to be made aware of the learning that is taking place. The targets should be shared with families to reinforce their understanding of learning activities in the classroom.

The following *I Can* statements are suggestions for learning targets and should be tailored to your children' abilities.

- ◆ *I can name five shapes.*
- ◆ *I can tell you what shapes look like.*
- ◆ *I can show what these words mean: above, below, beside, in front of, behind, and next to.*
- ◆ *I know that two-dimensional shapes are flat.*
- ◆ *I know that three-dimensional shapes are fat.*
- ◆ *I can find shapes at school and at home.*

Concluding Remarks

Once children have been exposed to the Mathematical Process Standards using some of the children's literature and hands-on materials from this book, choose other books and materials that can lend themselves to number sense, patterns, number relationships, measurement, and geometry concepts. Share ideas with your colleagues, start a list of books and materials with other teachers, and attend workshops or conferences related to early mathematical concepts. Continue growing the culture of mathematical problem solving at your school site by creating school-wide problem-solving situations, such as determining if there are more cars or trucks in the parking lot, counting the number of buses each day, or surveying if there are more children who like cats or dogs.

Post the child-friendly *I Can* statements in your class and send them home so children and families can refer to them throughout the year. Share problem-solving activities in newsletters, on the school or classroom website, at family events, and in the math work sent home. Continue to extend math concepts beyond the classroom by sending home activities (with examples and instructions) used in class so children can continue to practice concepts and skills.

Encourage administrators to purchase and house resources for incorporating problem solving in mathematics, such as professional books, periodicals, DVDs, games, hands-on materials, center activities, and children's literature. Collaborate with professionals at your site in order to integrate other content areas into math, such as art, music, and physical education. Act as a resource to support colleagues in their role as teachers of mathematics.

The following is a list of developmentally appropriate books recommended for each content area:

Number Sense

Accorsi, W. *10 button book*
Baker, K. *Potato Joe*
Carle, E. *The very hungry caterpillar*
Crews, D. *Ten black dots*
Falwell, C. *Feast for 10*
LeSieg, T. *Ten apples up on top!*
Litwin, E. *Pete the cat and his four groovy buttons*
McGrath, B. *Teddy bear counting*
Medina, J. *One big salad*
Milich, Z. *City 123*
Walsh, E.S. *Mouse count*

Patterns

Cleary, B. *ABABA: A book of pattern play*
Dahl, M. *Eggs and legs: Counting by twos*
Dahl, M. *Footprints in the snow: Counting by twos*
Dahl, M. *Pie for piglets: Counting by twos*
Dahl, M. *Hands down: Counting by fives*
Dahl, M. *Lots of ladybugs: Counting by fives*
Dahl, M. *Starry arms: Counting by fives*
Dahl, M. *Ants at the picnic: Counting by tens*
Dahl, M. *Bunches of buttons: Counting by tens*
Dahl, M. *Plenty of petals: Counting by tens*
Dahl, M. *Toasty toes: Counting by tens*
Harris, T. *Pattern bugs*
Harris, T. *Pattern fish*
McGrath, B. *Teddy bear patterns*
Murphy, S. *Beep beep, vroom vroom!*
Pluckrose, H. *Math counts: Pattern*

Number Relationships

Baker, K. *Quack and count*
Carle, E. *Rooster's off to see the world*
Garland, M. *How many mice?*
Norman, K. *Ten on the sled*
Sturges, P. *Ten flashing fireflies*
Tang, G. *Math fables*
Tang, G. *Math fables too*
Young, E. *Seven blind mice*

Measurement

Hoban, T. *Is it larger? Is it smaller?*
Hutchins, H. *A second is a hiccup: A child's book of time*
Jocelyn, M. *Sam sorts*
Jocelyn, M. *Hannah's collections*
Limentani, A. *How long is a whale?*
Limentani, A. *How much does a ladybug weigh?*
Mariconda, B. *Sort it out*
Pluckrose, H. *Math counts: Sorting*
Reid, M.S. *The button box*

Geometry

Aboff, M. *If you were a triangle*
Burns, M. *The greedy triangle*
Dodds, D. *The shape of things*
Gowler, R. *When a line bends . . . a shape begins*
Hall, M. *Perfect square*
Hoban, T. *Cubes, cones, cylinders, and spheres*
Hoban, T. *Shapes, shapes, shapes*
MacDonald, S. *Shape by shape*
Murry, D. *City shapes*
Stevenson, R.L. *Block city*
Walsh, E.S. *Mouse shapes*

The following is a list of materials used in each content chapter:

Materials	Number Sense	Patterns and Number Relationships	Measurement	Geometry
Number carpet	•			
Oversized number line	•			
Stickers	•			
Ink stamps	•			
Buttons	•		•	
Wooden blocks	•			
Pretend food/dishes	•			
Unifix cubes	•		•	
Pompoms	•			
Small plastic pool	•			
Magnetic/ wooden numbers	•			
Sand/play dough	•	•	•	•
Shaving cream/hair gel	•			
Learning links	•	•	•	
Chenille stems	•	•		•
Beads	•			
Bingo daubers	•	•		
Large dice	•			
Duplo blocks	•			
5 × 7 inch index cards	•	•		

Materials	Number Sense	Patterns and Number Relationships	Measurement	Geometry
Clear contact paper	•			
Paper/plastic placemats	•			
Chart paper	•			
Teddy bear/circle counters		•		
Lego		•	•	•
Pattern Blocks		•		•
Stuffed animals		•		
Tens frames		•		
Post-its		•		
Small containers		•	•	
Egg cartons		•		
Tinker toys		•	•	
Craft sticks		•	•	•
Bulletin board borders		•		
Cookie sheets		•		
Painter's tape		•		•
1-inch square tiles		•		
Dominoes		•		
Ice cube trays		•		
Waffle, foam, cardboard blocks		•		•
Pattern cards		•		•
Balance scale			•	

Materials	Number Sense	Patterns and Number Relationships	Measurement	Geometry
Linear calendars			•	
Rulers/tape measures/yard sticks			•	
String			•	
Feathers			•	
Shells			•	
Muffin tins			•	
Props for dramatic play			•	
Hula hoops			•	•
Toothpicks				•
Magna-tiles				•
Foam pool noodles				•
3D shapes				•
Tweezers				•
Straws				•
Hair rollers				•
Wiffle balls				•
Geoboards and rubber bands				•
Clothespins				•
Cookie cutters				•

Appendix
Sample Activity Plans

The following plans illustrate samples of activities embedded in daily routines for each of the mathematical concepts in this book. Use this format to create extension activities or repeat ideas provided within the content chapters.

Activity Plan for Number Sense

Routines: Circle time and sensory table.

Math skill: Recognizing and reciting numbers 1–10.

I Can statement (posted at students' eye level): *I can say numbers up to ten!*

Materials: Magnifying glasses, several number symbols (1–10) cut from construction paper or magnetic numbers placed around the classroom, several selections of children's literature: *Ten black dots, Feast for ten, Ten apples up on top!, Pete the cat and his four groovy buttons* placed in the circle.

Hook: Tell students they are going to be detectives to find clues to help solve a problem. They need to find numbers that go along with some of the books you have been reading in the classroom. What numbers can we find?

Instructional sequence:

◆ Direct instruction—Model using a magnifying glass and walk around the room to locate a number. Find a number, bring it back to the circle, and use positional words to describe the location of the numbers, such as "I found the number 5 *under* the light switch." Then match the number symbol to the numbers in one of the books.

◆ Guided practice—Ask for three to four "detectives" and allow them to get to work finding numbers around the classroom. Repeat the process until all of the students have found a number and have had an opportunity to match their number to the number symbol in one of the books.

◆ Independent practice—Place numbers on the sensory table and allow detectives to find the numbers and match them to numbers in the books. Then encourage the students to place the numbers on a large number line or number carpet.

◆ Scaffolding—Use magnetic numbers instead of paper numbers. The magnetic numbers will be easier to find, grasp, and carry.

Activity Plan for Patterning

Routine: Playground.

Math skill: Copy, describe, extend, and create a pattern with various modalities.

I Can statement (posted at students' eye level): *I can find and label a pattern.*

Materials: Safe play spaces outside the building, photos of areas around the school depicting patterns.

Hook: Show students photos of the neighborhood surrounding their school. Review some patterns they found inside their classroom. Tell them now they are going to find patterns outside of the school.

Instructional sequence:

◆ Direct instruction—Show students photos of the neighborhood and school building and point out patterns in the photos, such as:

Sidewalk—crack—sidewalk—crack
Window—brick—window—brick
Step—space—step—space (on a playground ladder)
Fence post—chain link—fence post—chain link

◆ Guided practice—Take a walk around the school and look for other patterns together as a class. Take photos of each student with the pattern they've discovered. Assemble the photos into a class book with the child's name and their pattern.

◆ Independent practice—Ask students to find patterns in their neighborhoods. Families can take a photo or help the child draw a picture of the patterns and send them to school to include in the class book.

◆ Scaffolding—Have photos of existing patterns ready for children to use if they are having difficulty locating a pattern.

Activity Plan for Measurement

Routine: Sensory table.

Math skill: Compare two objects in relation to each other.

I Can statement (posted at students' eye level): *I can use measurement vocabulary to solve a problem.*

Materials: A variety of cylinders (different length cardboard tubes), various sizes of marbles and small bouncy balls, painter's tape.

Hook: Share an oversized marble (ball) run with the students. Tell them they are going to experiment with the tubes to compare different-sized tunnels.

Instructional sequence:

◆ Direct instruction—Place different types of marble runs on the sensory table and show students how to test them to see which balls and marbles will travel through the cardboard tubes.

- ◆ Guided practice—Talk about which tubes are the longest and which ones are shorter.
- ◆ Independent practice—Show how to tape some tubes together to create different-sized tunnels. Who can create the longest tunnel? Which balls will travel through the tunnels? Students can create their own ball runs during play time.
- ◆ Scaffolding—Use plastic PVC pipes, cut at different lengths, with rubber balls.

Activity Plan for Geometry

Routine: Snack time.

Math skill: Recognize and name two and three-dimensional shapes.

I Can statement (posted at students' eye level): *I can create and name different shapes.*

Materials: Pretzel sticks, placemats, marshmallows.

Hook: Show students bags of marshmallows and pretzels and tell them they are going to use the snacks to construct the shapes they've been learning about in class.

Instructional sequence:

- ◆ Direct instruction—Use the pretzels to model how to place them together on the mat to create different shapes such as triangles, rectangles and squares. Then stick the pretzels into the marshmallows to create three-dimensional shapes such as a cube.
- ◆ Guided practice—Ask students to help you build a variety of two- and three-dimensional shapes with pretzels and marshmallows.
- ◆ Independent practice—Allow students to create their own shapes before they eat them.
- ◆ Scaffolding—Provide mats with shapes outlined on the surface so students can lay the pretzels on the outlines.

References

3D Shapes. (2015). Retrieved from http://lilcountrykindergarten.blogspot.com/

Aboff, M. (2009). *If you were a triangle*. Minneapolis, MN: Picture Window Books.

Accorsi, W. (1999). *10 button book*. New York: Workman Publishing.

Baker, K. (2004). *Quack and count*. Orlando, FL: Harcourt.

Beneke, S., Ostrosky, M., & Katz, L. (May, 2008). Calendar time for young children: Good intentions gone awry. *Young Children, 63*(3), 12–16.

Brett, J. (1996). *Goldilocks and the three bears*. New York: The Putnam & Grosset.

Carle, E. (1969). *The very hungry caterpillar*. New York: Philomel Books.

Carle, E. (1972). *Rooster's off to see the world*. New York: Simon & Schuster.

Christelow, E. (1989). *Five little monkeys jumping on the bed*. New York: Houghton Mifflin.

Christelow, E. (1993). *Five little monkeys sitting in a tree*. New York: Houghton Mifflin.

Crews, D. (1968). *Ten black dots*. New York: Greenwillow Books.

Dahl, M. (2004). *Lots of ladybugs: Counting by fives*. Mankato, MN: Picture Window Books.

Dahl, M. (2005). *Bunches of buttons: Counting by tens*. Mankato, MN: Picture Window Books.

Dahl, M. (2005). *Footprints in the snow: Counting by twos*. Mankato, MN: Picture Window Books.

de la Peña, M. (2015). *Last stop on Market Street*. New York: G.P. Putnam's Sons Books for Young Readers.

Ellis, C. (2015). *Home*. Cambridge, MA: Candlewick Press.

Falwell, C. (1993). *Feast for 10*. New York: Clarion Books.

Freeman, D. (1976). *Corduroy*. New York: Puffin Books.

Harris, T. (2000). *Pattern fish*. Minneapolis, MN: Millbrook Press.

Harris, T. (2001). *Pattern bugs*. Minneapolis, MN: Millbrook Press.

Hoban, T. (1986). *Shapes, shapes, shapes*. New York: Greenwillow Books.

Hutchins, H. (2007). *A second is a hiccup: A child's book of time*. New York: Arthur A. Levine Books.

Hyson, M. (2003). Putting early academics in their place. *Educational Leadership, 60*(7), 20–24.

Jocelyn, M. (2004). *Hannah's collections*. Toronto, Canada: Tundra Books.

Jocelyn, M. (2017). *Sam sorts*. Toronto, Canada: Tundra Books.

LeSieg, T. (1961). *Ten apples up on top!* New York: Random House.

Limentani, A. (2016). *How much does a ladybug weigh?* New York: Sterling.

Limentani, A. (2017). *How long is a whale?* New York: Sterling.

Litwin. E. (2012). *Pete the cat and his four groovy buttons*. New York: HarperCollins.

Murphy, S. (2000). *Beep beep, vroom vroom!* New York: Harper Collins.

NAEYC. (2009). *Where we stand on curriculum, assessment and program evaluation*. Position Statement. Washington DC: NAEYC.

NAEYC. (2010). *Early childhood mathematics: Promoting good beginnings*. Position Statement. Washington DC: NAEYC.

NCTM. (2000). *Principles and standards for school mathematics*. Reston, VA: NCTM.

NCTM. (October, 2013). *Mathematics in early childhood learning*. Position Statement. Reston, VA: NCTM.

Norman, K. (2010). *Ten on the sled*. New York: Sterling Children's Books.

Pinkney, J. (2017). *The three billy goats gruff*. New York: Little Brown Books.

Reid, M.S. (1990). *The button box*. New York: Puffin Unicorn Books.

SCALE. (2016). *edTPA early childhood assessment handbook*. Stanford, CA: Board of Trustees of the Leland Stanford Junior University.

Slobodkina, E. (2015). *Caps for sale*. New York: HarperCollins.

Southwest Institute for Families & Children (n.d.). *Say-Tell-Do-Play*.

Sturges, P. (1995). *Ten flashing fireflies*. New York: NorthSouth Books.

Taback, S. (1997). *There was an old lady who swallowed a fly*. New York: Viking Press.

Tang, G. (2004). *Math fables*. New York: Scholastic.

Tang, G. (2007). *Math fables too*. New York: Scholastic.

Walsh, E. (2007). *Mouse shapes*. Orlando, FL: Harcourt.

Weston, A. (1993). *Eenie, meenie, miney, math!* Boston, MA: Little, Brown.

Wood, A. (1984). *The napping house*. Orlando, FL: Harcourt.

Young, E. (1992). *Seven blind mice*. New York: Scholastic.